Letters Home
A Soldier's Legacy

Roger L. Shaffer

Republic of Texas Press

Library of Congress Cataloging-in-Publication Data

Shaffer, Roger L. (Roger Lee), 1941-
   Letters home : a soldier's legacy / Roger L. Shaffer.
      p.   cm.
   Text is interwoven with letters written home from the Army by the
author's uncle, William (Bill) A. Rogers.
   Includes bibliographical references.
   ISBN 1-55622-488-5 (pbk.)
   1. Rogers, William A., 1918-1944--Correspondence.   2. World War,
1939-1945--Personal narratives, American.   3. United States. Army-
-Biography   4. Soldiers--United States--Correspondence.
   I. Rogers, William A., 1918-1944.   II. Title.
D811.D4598   1996
940.54'8173--dc20   96-11712
                                      CIP

Republic of Texas Press is an imprint of Wordware Publishing, Inc.
No part of this book may be reproduced in any form or by any means
without permission in writing from Wordware Publishing, Inc.

Printed in the United States of America

ISBN 1-55622-488-5
10 9 8 7 6 5 4 3 2 1
9608

All inquiries for volume purchases of this book should be addressed to
Wordware Publishing, Inc., at 1506 Capital Avenue, Plano, Texas 75074.
Telephone inquiries may be made by calling:

(214) 423-0090

Now it is April and spring comes softly over winter weary hills touching them with light fingers of green.
Last year my heart was happy, dancing with every sunbeam. Now it is dead. Dead with the boy who knew Italian winter's cold and rain and lies 'neath alien skies never to see another spring.

Ivy Rogers

Contents

Preface

On September 15, 1944, the *Billings Gazette*, Billings, Montana, ran the following article:

Posthumous D. S. C. Awarded

Edgar Lieutenant Was Killed in Italy

Washington, Sept. 15.—(*P*)—Posthumous award of the distinguished service cross to Lieutenant William A. Rogers of Edgar, Mont., out outstanding action in Italy, was announced Friday by the war department.

Lieutenant Rogers, son of Mrs. Ivy A. Rogers of Edgar, was killed last January 28.

The citation read:

"Leading a four-man reconnaisance patrol, Lieutenant Rogers crossed a treacherous river and moved forward over the heavily mined terrain under continuous fire of the enemy. Although pinned down on several occasions by concentrated mortar and machine-gun fire, he continued his advance, deploying his men and gathering the information essential to his mission. Remaining in this hazardous area until a thorough reconnaisance was completed, he returned to lead his battallion in a swift assault on the objectives he had scouted."

I was not yet three years old when my uncle, Lt. William A. Rogers, was killed. Aside from family anecdotes, I never knew him. Forty-five years after his death I acquired eighty-one letters he had written home during his army days. The letters begin on his first day in the army and end just six days before his death. I came to know my uncle Bill through those letters and through meeting and corresponding with the officers and men he served with. So will the reader. What a rewarding experience it is. Bill was typical of the fine young men called upon by their country during the war. Typical, yet, like all who served in those trying times, very special.

Acknowledgments

Without the unselfish support of those men who came home after the war, this work would be incomplete. Charles W. Stimson, Evan MacIlraith, Gerhard Rehder, Mabene Allen, J.B. Worley, Jim Henson, E. E. Carter, Clifford Hale, Welden Green, Johnnie Pricer, Charles L. Hearn, Red Morgan, Wood Jenkins, John Johnson and Terrell J. Davis added immeasurably to an understanding of Bill Rogers and the times. My thanks to the 36th Division Association, the family of General Walker, and to Mr. Robert W. Wagner for their generous permission to use portions of *The Fighting 36th*, *From Texas to Rome* and *The Texas Army*. Finally, a special thanks to my family for their support and guidance.

RLS

I
The Eve of War
and the Rogers Family

On the eve of World War II America was a country bitterly divided. Despite worldwide turmoil following the rise of Hitler and Mussolini and the savage Japanese aggression in China, in the thirties, isolationists controlled the Congress. Powerful men like Charles Lindberg, Henry Ford, and Joseph P. Kennedy were very influential in keeping America neutral and unentangled. It wasn't until the fall of 1939, after Germany invaded Poland (and France and England, finally recognizing that appeasement was a policy failure, declared war on Germany) that the American Neutrality laws were amended to allow the Allies to purchase—cash-and-carry—the weapons and munitions necessary to resist the onslaught. The ammendment still took a special session of Congress and six weeks of debate.

Americans only watched as the European situation deteriorated. In the spring of 1940 Hitler's famous *blitzkrieg* tactics easily took Denmark, Norway, the Netherlands, Belgium, Luxembourg, and France. England was now alone against Germany. Things got worse. First there was Dunkirk. Then, in the summer of 1940, Hitler sent the Luftwaffe against England.

Our own national security was tenuous, and the shift to military preparedness came slowly. On July 20, 1940, Roosevelt signed the Navy Expansion Act. On August 27, 1940, Congress authorized the call to active duty, for one year, of the National Guard[1] and the Reserves. Then, finally, after considerable debate, Congress passed the first peacetime draft in American history.

On September 16, 1940, the Burke-Wadsworth Selective Service and Training Act was signed into law. Under the Act all men between 21 and 35 years of age were required to register for the draft and were subject to one year of military training.

The draft came none too soon. On September 27, 1940, Japan, Germany, and Italy signed the Tripartite Pact, dividing the world between them and promising to come to each other's aid should they be attacked "by a power not presently involved in the European war or in the Sino-Japanese conflict." By this they meant the United States. The Tripartite Pact sought to intimidate America into doing nothing, because movement against one would mean war with all.

THE ROGERS FAMILY

In 1899, just twenty-three years after Custer was killed, William A. Sutton moved his wife, Eva, and their two daughters, six-year-old Bessie and three-year-old Ivy, from Utica, Montana to land he purchased from the Indians at Rockvale, Montana, seventy miles west of the Little Big Horn battle site. He built a cabin and started clearing the land for farming. That first winter Bessie and Ivy both came down with diphtheria. Bessie died. Ivy recovered and two years later brother Frank was born. Sister Wynn rounded out the family ten years later.

Sometime after the Suttons began farming at Rockvale, Donald Rogers and his younger brother Andrew came from Michigan and homesteaded land nearby. In addition to farming, Donald took on the job of teaching at the one-room

---

1   An event later to be of significance to Bill Rogers occurred on November 25, 1940 when the Texas National Guard was inducted into the Federal Service. It became the 36th Division and began the training necessary to bring it to combat readiness.

school in Rockvale. Ivy was one of his students. But it was the younger Andrew Rogers that captured her attention.

On August 29, 1915, nineteen-year-old Ivy Alice Sutton married Andrew William Rogers at her parent's farm in Rockvale. Shortly thereafter Ivy and "Rog" moved to the Rogers' family farm in Hillsdale, Michigan. There, on August 23, 1916, their first child, my mother Jeanne, was born. To support their now growing family, Rog and Ivy moved to Detroit. While there were occasional trips to Montana, the Rogers lived in Detroit for the next twenty years, and the rest of their children, Bill, Dorothy, and Don, were all born and raised there.

A good student and an avid reader, Bill Rogers played trumpet in local dance bands, was interested in photography, and wrote songs and poetry. Although not a big man at just five foot five and 132 pounds, he was physical, competitive, and fearless. He accepted all challenges, intellectual as well as physical, with enthusiasm. He made friends easily. With his infectious humor, natural good looks (brown hair, blue eyes), and engaging manner, he was popular with the young ladies too.

On her father's death Ivy inherited the Montana property, and in 1937 the entire family moved to Rockvale to take up farming. Jeanne returned to Detroit and in 1938 married my father, Al Shaffer. Dorothy married Don Bolenske, a Montana farmer. Rog and Ivy later divorced and Rog left Montana. Ivy took a job at Mount Aqua, a mineral bath resort near Rockvale, and thus it came to be that Bill Rogers, a graduate of Detroit's Redford High School, was farming in Montana on the eve of World War II.

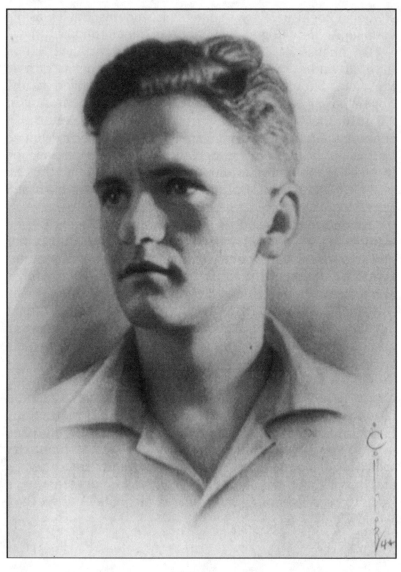

Bill Rogers
(18-20 years old)

The "Little House" Rockvale, Montana

At the Rogers' farm Rockvale, Montana 1939. From left: "Rog," Bill Rogers, Cousin Mary Lee Rogers, Donnie Rogers, Ivy, and Uncle Don Rogers.

II
I've Been Accepted

Across America the draft began. On February 14, 1941, the Selective Service Local Board at Red Lodge, Montana notified Bill Rogers that he was classified as I-A. Five days later, and just ten days before his twenty-third birthday, Bill was inducted into the army at Fort Missoula, Montana. He wrote home regularly.

Feb. 19, 1941

Dear Mom,

I've been accepted. Passed all the exams easily. We have to be sworn in tonight and again in the morning. We leave for Fort Lewis at Tacoma at 3:00 P.M. tomorrow.

We had a nice ceremony at Red Lodge and left on the bus at 6:30 P.M. Arrived in Billings at 8:15 P.M. Had dinner at Uncle Sam's expense. Entrained at midnight for Missoula. We actually got pullmans but they didn't do us much good because some of the fellows had whiskey and made so much noise that the rest of us couldn't sleep. It will be different going to Fort Lewis tho, because an officer will be in charge of us.

Had breakfast on the train. Red Stephenson and I are hanging together pretty well. We shared a lower berth on the train and have adjoining beds in the barracks. Our first meal was the awfullest mess that I ever ate. Cold beans, under done potatoes—and Jello with beans in it.

We're waiting now to be sworn in and then will eat and have a bath.

My regards to Tom and Edith.

Bill

Feb. 27, 1941
Co. C. 15th Inf.
Fort Lewis, Washington

Dear Mom,

We have been stationed in permanent quarters at last. Have not been issued all our clothes yet but what we have got fit very well. We've got pretty good officers, and the best mess sergeant in the Army. We really get good food.

I know quite a bit about drill and the corporal uses me for demonstration purposes and sometimes I drill the awkward squad. Tom can explain this to you. By the way tell Tom and Edith hello for me and tell him I think I like the Army. We're in quarantine yet. We can't mix with the regular army.

Don't like this country right now. It's still winter and rains every day. It's supposed to be summer in about a month.

There are 60 of us in this barracks, 32 upstairs and 28 down. I'm upstairs.

Most of the fellows are pretty nice but there are two or three dumb ones who are holding the rest of us back on drill.

We are going to have to smell mustard gas and Lewisite gas later. Don't think I'm going to like that.

We will get rifles in a few days.

Have to make our beds each morning. Tear them down to the mattress and turn it over. Tom probably can tell you about this too.

Guess that's about all for now.

Bill

March 8, 1941
Co. C. 15th Inf.
Fort Lewis, Washington

Dear Mom,

I'll answer your questions first.
1. The hay was $3.50 per ton and we figured that there was five (5) tons of it left. We bought 10.

2. I don't know where the teaspoons are. Dorothy might.
3. Don't know anything about the glove.

I got your first letter o.k.

I'm to be company bugler. I'll get a "private first class" rating right away and will make $36.00 a month instead of $21.00. Maybe not the first month or two.

Send me Dad's address when you get it. Also send me Chris' address as soon as he sends it to you.

I wrote to Frank at 111 Marston. Was that the correct address?

Had a letter from uncle Don. He can't get up this way so I won't see him while I'm here but I may get stationed in California after our training is over.

We are being instructed very intensively. We've had close order drill, extended order drill, military courtesy and can take a Garand M1 rifle apart and put it together in considerably less than a minute.

Our shoes—army, civilian and bedroom slippers are polished every day.

We got a good fit on our clothes. Will send pictures sometime if I can get my hands on a camera.

The rain seems to have cleared up.

We had a big Army review yesterday. The stand was full of Generals and the Mayors of Tacoma and Seattle and the Gov. of Washington were there. We recruits didn't march. We sat on the hill right next to the stand. 3,250 of us.

The rubber hose is in the kitchen of the Dutch house. The lariat was broken and so we used it for halter ropes.

Glad you're getting along so well. I'm sure satisfied. Don't know yet but I may re-enlist at the end of my year.

Tell Tom that he can have the shotgun for $20.00 if he wants it.

Glad I brought my slippers along I wear them every evening.

We got our 3rd typhoid shot today. We're out of quarantine now.

Bill

"We got a good fit on our clothes." Ft. Lewis, Washington.

While America's new draftees took their shots and learned about army life, the British continued to fight and now faced a new problem, cash-and-carry. Following Dunkirk, and on an emergency basis, the President had shipped Britain all available weapons. Later, fifty destroyers were exchanged for Atlantic coast naval bases. But now our cash-and-carry policy for war supplies was a problem. The war was draining away British funds, and in December 1940 London announced she was running out of money. As a solution, on January 10, 1941, the Roosevelt Administration introduced the "lend-lease" bill.

Lend-lease allowed the President to give aid, in the form of war material and other supplies, to any nation whose defense he believed vital to the United States. Repayment could be "in kind or property, or any other direct or indirect benefit which the President deems satisfactory." That latitude would make the United States at least an economic partner against Germany. Naturally, this major policy change was bitterly contested. However, on March 11, 1941 the bill was signed into law and America began to earn its title, "the arsenal of democracy."

While such major policy changes would affect their lives soon, the draftees' world view was still somewhat narrow, and army life was beginning to grow a little tiresome.

March 27, 1941

Dear Butch,

Here's the letter I owe you. Just got one from Dad and wrote to him. Suggested that he pay the fifty but I doubt that he will.

I hate to say this, but you'd think me very rude if I didn't thank you. So I'd better say it. The money wasn't in the letter. If you want to send me something send a book. But don't do it if you're short of money.

Glad the job is easy enough and that you are having a little fun. You sure had your share of grief these past years.

It would seem from your reports that Tom is preparing to do a job of farming. Did he say anything about buying the shotgun?

Had a letter from Chris and wrote to him. Should see him in the near future.

If you see Maxine tell her I'm sorry but I haven't had time to work on those tunes of hers. We're kept pretty busy.

Oh! By the way—it never occurred to me until one of the other fellows had to inform his mother. This business about hostesses is a lot of bunk. There are just three stationed at Fort Lewis to arrange dances for the men, and there are 40,000 men here, so you see our chance of getting to a dance are pretty slim.

I've been asked to try out for the band and I think I can make it.

I'm getting along alright but it's getting pretty monotonous.

If you send me a book I'd like the collected works of Nietzsche. I'll send you the difference if it costs more.

Regards
Bill

P.S. I seem to be getting over that perpetual cold of mine.

B

"Chris" was Chris Jenson, a Rockvale area friend. Chris and Percy Hopper, another Rockvale friend, came to Washington State and got defense jobs in the Seattle area. Chris ended up in the army later.

April 7, 1941

Dear Mom,

I'm sending the money back and I want you to get me a book with it. If it takes more let me know.

I tried out for the band and I think I made it.

Had a bad cough and cold and sore throat last week but got over it o.k. except that I'm a little hoarse.

Went to Renton over the weekend and saw Chris and Percy. Had a swell time.

I think you'd like this state. Every house in Seattle looks as tho a landscape gardener had built the grounds around it. All kinds of colors.

We have finished recruit drill and are going to be turned to duty in a few days. Our company commander who was a 1st Lieutenant has been promoted to Captain and is going to throw a party for the whole company next Sat. at Bremerton.

Would appreciate any magazines you could send. (NOT LIFE). Am sending Donnie a couple of books. Will send them to you and you give them to him.

Bill

LIFE had been showing pictures of the Luftwaffe's bombing attacks on England. Anxious for a complete victory, immediately after the fall of France, Hitler began planning operation "Sea Lion," the invasion of England.

But England had not been successfully invaded since the Norman Conquest in 1066, and it was not to happen now.[1] The Royal Air Force was magnificent. And, despite the massive bombing, the indomitable spirit of the English people— described so eloquently by Churchill as "their finest hour" —was a factor never understood by Hitler. That spirit, the R.A.F., and a brand new technology called "radar" combined to deny Hitler a victory in England. After losing the Battle of Britain the former corporal turned his attention elsewhere.

---

1 The British Channel Islands could not be defended and were occupied by the Germans from July 1, 1940, until the end of the war.

On June 22, 1941, in what is often characterized as a repeat of another little corporal's famous military error, Hitler began a two-front war when he attacked Russia without having defeated Britain. Many Americans were not sympathetic with Russia. Perhaps because in 1939 Russia signed a nonaggression pact with Germany and they divided Poland between them. Roosevelt and Churchill, however, saw it as another opportunity to defeat Hitler, the greater evil. Roosevelt extended lend-lease to Russia.

Meanwhile, all too aware of their own uncertain future, America's draftees tried to make plans for themselves and look after things at home.

July 18, 1941

Dear Mom,

Thanks a lot for the pictures. I guess I do owe you a letter so here it is.

Spent the last two weekends in Seattle with Don, Lauretta and Lee. Had a fine time and met a great many people whom they know. Talked with Don quite a long while about attending Washington U. Nothing definite of course because of the uncertainty of the future, but I may go.

Don't know for sure where the car papers are but you might try the letter file that I used to keep in the bunk house, or possibly they are in the buffet drawer. By the way, please send me one of my little photo albums (an empty one) and also my copy of "Rain In The Doorway."

I'm trying to get a transfer to Regimental Headquarters Co. The commanding officer (Major Renfro) said that he would take me. Now all I have to do is get a release from my C.O., which may be pretty difficult. Keep your fingers crossed for me. If I can transfer I may be able to study radio or else get a motorcycle job.

Last night a kid named Allen and I went to Tacoma and I bought a quart of wine, its unbelievably cheap, and then drank it sitting on a bench in a little park while we talked about Detroit. He used to live on Linwood and Davison. We're planning to go to Point Defiance Park just out of Tacoma this Sunday and go swimming.

Lauretta just had an operation for tumor on her left shoulder. The surgeon did a fine job and it shouldn't even leave much of a scar.

Looks as tho I were going to be kept in more than a year but I'm going to try to get home at Christmas time.

When was the picture of Dor and Don taken? He looks pretty big thru the middle.

The lights are going out so good bye for now.

Love,
Bill

Sat.

Am sending a snap I had taken on the ocean park pier at Venice, California.

B.

Bill and the 115th Regiment had been in California on strike duty. North American Aviation's plant at Inglewood, California was one of the country's two main producers of fighter aircraft. On June 5, 1941, 4,000 union workers went on strike, ringed the plant, and turned back police attempts to break their picket lines. Washington was determined to crack down on defense plant strikes. When attempts to negotiate a return to work failed and strike demonstrations increased, President Roosevelt, by executive order, authorized the army to seize the plant and break the strike. On June 9, 1941, 2,500 troops, Bill included, moved in with fixed bayonets. They were effective.

On July 19, 1941, Bill's sister Jeanne and her husband Al welcomed into the troubled world their second son, Roger Lee Shaffer.

With the world situation deteriorating it became clear to the President and others that American security required the draftee's "one year" terms be extended. Army Chief of Staff General George C. Marshall worried that release of the trainees would bring about a disintegration of the army that might "well involve a national tragedy." A bill was introduced. The

Isolationists, not yet convinced, fought against the extension. Meanwhile, Roosevelt and Churchill met at sea off the coast of Newfoundland and formulated the "Atlantic Charter." The bill passed the Senate, but only after vigorous debate. Then, on August 12, 1941, and by just one vote, the House of Representatives passed the Service Extension Act of 1941. Thus, by that one vote, a short four months before Pearl Harbor, America narrowly averted the devastating setback of the loss of its body of trained men.

The Service Extension Act also provided for hardship discharges for men with dependents, and eligibility for discharge for men over twenty-eight.

Military training was stepped up too. In August 1941, in what was touted as the largest peacetime maneuvers in the history of the United States, draftees and activated guardsmen took part in training designed to simulate war conditions and test men and equipment. At Fort Lewis more than 10,000 officers and men took part in the largest command post maneuvers ever held in the west.

August 29, 1941

Dear Mom,

I'm getting a furlough. It will start Sept. 8th so I should be home about the 10th or 11th. I'm going to hitch hike. I'll stay at the Dutch house but will come to Mt. Aqua first to see you. I'm going to get 20 days so I figure on working about two weeks. I want to get enough money to buy a cheap motorcycle. It costs too much out here to go anywhere when you have to take the bus. 90 cents just to go to Seattle.

I suppose you have read about the maneuver we just held. It was pretty easy until the last three days. It rained then steadily and we only got about two hours sleep a night.

Had a letter from Jean. She is fine. Will write to Dad in a few days.

All the fellows in the company who have dependents or are over 28 years old are getting out in the near future. They signed some papers about it today. Maybe they won't keep us the 2 1/2 years.

Just got a letter and a picture from Mary Lee. She's
getting to be awfully cute. Still spoiled tho.

Wonder what Don will say when I tell him I sold the
Moon.

Guess that's all for now.

See you soon
Love, Bill

The "Moon" was an old car given to Bill by his uncle,
Donald Rogers. At one time the car had been Uncle Don's
pride and joy.

Bill, along with Ray Allen, his soldier friend from Detroit,
came to Montana and enjoyed a furlough. Ray's mother joined
them. There was an outing to Billings with both Ray's mother
and Ivy. The snapshots show Bill and Ray with both the proud
mothers.

Left to right:
Ray's mother,
Ray, Ivy.

Left to right:
Ray's mother,
Bill, Ivy.

Oct. 4, 1941

Dear Mom,

I've been back at the Fort for a week. Had a good trip.
Spent Wednesday and Thursday at McKenzies. We rode
all day Thursday. Took a lot of pictures but haven't had
them developed yet. It only takes 25 hrs. to make the bus
trip. Had to pay full fare tho ($16.55) so I had to use your
money. I was gone when the payroll was signed so I
didn't get paid this month. May get paid on the tenth or
not till next month. Unless you need the money I'll
probably send it 5 dollars at a time. I want to put 20
dollars a month in postal savings. Decided that I'm going
to go to college.

I'm bugler now and should start drawing 36.00 per.

Signed up for a photography course and for night
school but may not go. Think I have a chance to work in
the Sergeant's Club here on the post. If I can get the job it
will help pay my first year in college.

Have a letter from Jean. Says that if I'm still in the
army next summer that she will be out for a visit. I expect
to get out in Feb. but if I have any place to put her would
like her to come anyway.

Wrote to Frank but the letter came back marked "not
at that address"—111 Marston.

Saw Lum and Clara in Laurel before I left.

Have a lot of letters to write so I'll have to close now.

Love,
Bill

Oct. 27, 1941

Dear Mom,

Not much time to write but thought I'd let you know
that I'm still alive. This bugler job is a snap and I'm
spending a lot of my spare time at the photography club.
Some of my furlough pictures are excellent will send you
copies right after payday. Have to wait till then to get
more paper for prints.

Ed Sevihart invited me to Kelso for the weekend and I
went with him. He had a blind date all fixed up for me

and as she was a pretty blond I had a swell time. May go back again to see her. Took some pictures and if they're good will send some.

All discharges have been stopped temporarily. Don't know when I'll get out for sure.

Had a letter from Red. He's very well satisfied in California, but I think that he signed up for three years.

Will get a ten day furlough at Christmas and I think I'll invite myself down to uncle Don's.

Hope you either sell the place or get a good renter on it.

Love,
Bill

Nov. 7, 1941

Dear Mom,

Enclosed are a couple of pictures I thought you might like to have. Someday I'll tell you who all the rest of the fellows are.

Cpl. Morris of this co. was killed in a car accident night before last. I have to play "taps" at his funeral. He slept second bunk to mine.

Was only able to save $10 dollars this month but I got all my debts paid including seven dollars to Chet Jenson I had forgotten I owed him. (He worked for me a while in Montana.)

I'm going to night school now. Studying trigonometry.

Have a girlfriend at last, but she lives about a hundred miles from here so I don't get to see her much. It's nothing serious. Just someone to dance with. Blond and about two inches taller than I am.

More pictures later. Time to fall out now.

Love
Bill

"Ed Sevihart invited me to
Kelso . . . he had a blind date all
fixed up . . . and as she was a
pretty blond I had a swell time."

Bill Rogers far right. "Enclosed are a couple of pictures . . . someday I'll tell you who all the rest of the fellows are."

"Don't know whether you picked me out in the band picture or not. I'm playing a bugle, not my trumpet. I'm on the far side toward the rear and all but my head and shoulders is behind a big bass horn."

Nov. 22, 1941

Dear Mom,

Don't know whether you picked me out in the band picture or not. I'm playing a bugle, not my trumpet. I'm on the far side toward the rear and all but my head and shoulders is behind a big bass horn.

Glad to hear that Donnie is going to live with Dorothy. It will be better for him. Had a letter from him this week. He says that you are apt to sell the place soon now. I hope so. It has become such a headache. After I get out of the army, I'm pretty sure I can go to work for $40 or $50 a week. Wages are awfully high out here. Do you think you might like to come out here and live with me?

Don't know whether I have a girl in Kelso or not. I've never been down to see her after that first time so she may be sore at me.

I got the candy o.k. and it was swell but I thought Jean sent it and I wrote her a thank you letter. Did you send it or did you both send some and only one got here? The candy I got was fudge with nuts in it and very good too. Just in case it was you and not Jean that sent it: thanks a lot.

Spent Thanksgiving in town. Went to a high school football game.

Glad you liked the shampoo. It's good stuff.

I'm getting along rapidly in my night school work. Will finish this course on Dec. 18th and will probably take a course in physics then.

See if you can locate Ray Allen on the picture. I'm running around with him now.

Had a nice letter from Bettie. I think she's beginning to soften up a little. It's going to be pretty tough on me if someone else gets her. I've never met another girl that could begin to take her place. I think I'm a one woman man.

Wrote to Dad but haven't heard from him. I think he has a new address but I'm not sure.

Our first Sergeant (Emery, he is not in the picture) has been transferred to Schofield Barracks Oahu, Hawaii.

Captain Lafferty is transferring to the Ski regiment and Lt. O'Neil is the new company commander. He is a good guy.

Just happened to think! I sent a picture to Bettie and one to you. Whose did I write the names on the back of? Yours I think.

That's all for now.

Love
Bill

Bettie was a girl from Bill's Detroit high school days. She and her friend Jean Boyle were close family friends of the Rogers and Shaffers. Bill's feelings are clear.

III
War

On December 7, 1941, the Japanese effectively ended apathy and isolationism in America. In the President's famous "date which will live in infamy" message he told Americans that in addition to attacking American naval and military forces in the Hawaiian Islands, the Japanese had attacked Hong Kong, Guam, the Philippines, Wake Island, and Midway Island. He went on to say: "No matter how long it may take us to overcome this premeditated invasion, the American people in their righteous might will win through to absolute victory...As Commander in Chief of the Army and Navy I have directed that all measures be taken for our defense."

Dec. 7, 1941

Dear Mom,

I'm writing this letter from Buckley's in Redmond. We've had the news and have been ordered by radio to return to the fort. I wanted to write once more before they start censoring our mail. I guess we'll be leaving before long but don't know when or from where. When I do find out I don't suppose I'll be allowed to tell you. Don't worry about me. I know how to take care of myself and it will be at least several months before I see any real action. We'll probably go to Manila or Shanghai.

Tell everyone good bye for me and I wish I could see them again before I leave. Tell the kid I haven't time to write now but may have later.

Don't send me any Christmas presents because I don't want you to spend your money. I have everything I need and you have so many expenses. I've really got plenty of

money for what little I need and I wouldn't feel right
about accepting presents when you're so hard up.

I've got to go now so good bye and don't worry.

Love
Bill

Enraged by the Japanese sneak attack, American men by
the thousands refused to wait for the draft and jammed army
and navy recruiters. Some recruiters even opened that Sunday. Those draftees already in the army were eager to fight.
There was also a fear of saboteurs among us and of a Japanese attack on the west coast of the United States.

Formal alignment of the Allied and Axis powers began.
Immediately following our declaration of war against Japan,
Great Britain and those governments-in-exile forced out of
their own countries by the invading Germans also declared
war against Japan. Then, on December 11, 1941, Germany
and Italy honored their obligations under the Tripartite Pact
and declared that a state of war with the United States existed,
whereupon Congress promptly declared war upon them as
well.

Dec. 13, 1941

Dear Mom,

I'm sending all my civilian clothes to you because we
are no longer allowed to wear or have them. If the kid
can use any of them he is welcome to them. The
gladstone should be handy if you visit Wynn this winter.

Monday night we left the fort and bivouacked in the
woods until the Navy had made sure that no Jap ships
were near enough to the coast to launch a bomber attack.
Came in Friday after a very miserable week of rain.

Still don't know where we're going or if we're going
anywhere. Had our blood typed today. I'm type A.

Capt. Billings has returned to the company and is
once again our company commander. For which thanks
be. He's a martinet, but he knows what he's doing and
we know where we stand.

We had a practice air raid alarm at 11:00 A.M.

I've got 80 rounds of ammunition in my rifle belt and it stays there at all times. We sleep in our clothes and keep our rifles by our beds. Just a precautionary measure however.

Your letter just came and I was sure glad to hear from you. Yes, I'm glad that I'm in the army now that we have declared war. Hope we get to go across. We haven't been told a thing tho, so I don't know whether there's any chance or not.

I have made out a pay allotment to you. It's for fifteen dollars a month. If you need it it's yours to spend and I'd sure like to have you use it to help pay for your trip to Texas. If you haven't any use for it, let it pile up or buy some defense bonds with it and I'll have a nest egg when I get discharged.

Hope Don can go to Dad. I think that it would do him a lot of good besides helping him. Tell him if there's anything of mine at home that he wants he's welcome to it.

(Good luck Donnie and keep your nose clean.)

Bettie and Jean Boyle each wrote me a letter last Sunday when the news came over the radio and right now you couldn't put a dent in my morale with a post maul.

Today I got Christmas presents from both of them. I guess a little "war hysteria" is a good ingredient to add to luke warm romance.

Hope you can dispose of the farm.

We haven't been able to go anywhere where I can buy Christmas presents so I don't know what I'm going to do unless I get to buy some later. Haven't had a chance to send my clothes yet (they're all packed) but I guess I will later.

I'm as healthy as a spring colt and weigh about 125 now. Maybe if this war goes on long enough, the army will succeed in making a man out of me.

Love
Bill

Ivy's planned trip to Texas was to visit her sister, Wynn, and Wynn's husband, Pearl Olds, in Houston.

Dec. 28, 1941

Dear Mom,

Your package arrived yesterday. The candy, especially the penuche, was swell. Haven't had any good home made candy since that box you sent before. Got some candy from Jean and Dor and uncle Don and from Dad too but none of it was fudge.

I finally opened your first package the day before Christmas. Thanks a million for the swell gift. It's exactly what I need. I had bought myself a fishing tackle box to keep my things in but it was much too bulky to be convenient. The empty bag is perfect. I can keep what I need in it and don't have to carry something along that I don't want, just because it's in the set.

Maybe you'd like to hear what I received for Christmas. Dad sent me a very nice box. It contained a billfold made of <u>glass</u>, a carton of cigarettes and an assortment of candy and nuts.

Dor and Don sent me a box of cookies, candy and cigarettes.

Jean and Al sent me a box of candied dates and a shaving kit and a framed picture of Jean which is now displayed very prominently in my foot locker.

Don and Lauretta sent me a box of candy and cigarettes.

Mrs. Buckley in Redmond sent Ray Allen and I each a box of cookies and candy.

My face hasn't broken out yet from eating so much sweet stuff, but it probably will.

I finally got two gross (288 sheets) of print paper. If we stay here long enough I'll have a bunch of pictures for you.

Expect to leave here soon but mail addressed to me here will be forwarded so don't wait to write.

Almost forgot. Jean Boyle sent me a Christmas copy of Esquire and a beautiful calendar made of pictures of the Vargas girl. And Bettie sent me a carton of Camels.

That's all for now. Write soon.

Love,
Bill

P.S. Could you send me some assorted buttons. I've got a sewing kit but it is almost impossible to get buttons.

Jan. 13, 1942

Dear Mom

Not much to write about but I thought I'd write anyway.

Had a letter from Dad. He says he is going to send for Don soon. He figures on going to work for Dupont making shells.

Heard from Jean too. She is fine and the kids are both o.k.

I'm going to regimental intelligence school every day now. We study map reading—compass work—sketching—scouting and patrolling etc. Very interesting.

You say that you heard from Chris. Well when you write to him tell that I'm sore at him and Percy too. Neither one of them has ever come to see me here at the fort. It wasn't so bad when I could get weekends off but now that passes are limited to six hours, I never get to see anyone. Tacoma is as far as we can go on a six hr leave and I don't know anyone there.

I was going to send you some pictures but I guess I'll wait. I'm filling my big album and when it is finished I will send it to you.

My friend Allen received a corporal's rating, so some of us went to Tacoma Sunday night and wet down his stripes.

Oh Yes! Mrs. Buckley is the wife of Frank Buckley—mother of Roy Buckley—Frank owns a gas station in Redmond and is on the local council and evacuation committee. Mrs. Buckley (Margaret) is an air raid warden. Roy is a student at Wash. University and is a member of R.O.T.C.

Collectively they are one of Don and Lauretta's oldest friends in Seattle.

That's all I have time for now.

Love,
Bill

"Duncan," mentioned in the next letter, is Elmer Duncan, the local administrator for the latest version of "New Deal" farm loans. Administration was somewhat informal in Rockvale, but the Rogers believed in repaying their loans.

Jan. 26, 1942

Dear Mom,

As near as I can remember we waited until you had returned to give the money to Duncan. If you'll recall, I took the money up to him several times and he kept telling me that maybe I'd better hang onto it for awhile. You kept the money in that small brown purse of yours. I think that when the money was finally paid that you took it up.

The amounts (110.-48.-53) are correct or nearly so. Just happened to think—didn't you pay Dunc right in the kitchen? It was raining that day and he stopped by on his way to Red Lodge. Hope that you can get everything straightened out.

Glad Dodo's well—she was not feeling so good when I was there on furlough. Sorry but I haven't seen any of the people you mentioned in your other letter. This fort is like a city (60,000) and there is no directory. Besides we are kept busy almost all of the time. My outfit is on the alert again, which means that for 48 hours we sleep, eat and live in our clothes.

Wait just a little longer and I'll send you that album and then you'll have all the pictures you want.

Just had another thought—it's been so long that it's hard to remember clearly. Was that money deposited in the Fromberg Bank and used by Chris and me to buy feed and seed? If so—then when Dunc came thru with the feed and seed money that he was supposed to furnish us—the money was paid back. Remember when we were ready to thresh and the money finally came thru and we joked about it because the crop it was supposed to plant was ready for harvesting.

You'll find all my own receipts in that old letter file unless it has been cleaned out.

Yes one of the suitcase clasps was broken. If the trumpet is in the way you can send it to Jean. She said that she would keep it for me, but when I got ready to send it, I didn't have her address. If you don't need it, Don can have the suitcase to make the trip East.

Wish him luck for me. He'll be a good kid as soon as he gets a few more years under his hat.

I looked up my record today and on the army general classification test I made a score of 149. As far as I know only one man in the regiment (3,000 men) did better. He made 150. Didn't know that your son was so smart did you? A score of 128 is above average.

Had a tooth pulled today and will have a couple filled on the 8th of February.

A letter from Frank today, he is his usual zany self. Said he had heard from you.

From the reports, we're finally beginning to strike back at the Japanese, 7 ships sunk over the weekend.

Don't use the allotment money for bonds yet. Cash the checks and hang onto the money. I may need it urgently in a few months. Can't tell you why yet because I'm not sure and don't want to talk about it till I am, but it isn't going overseas so you don't have to worry about that.

Love,
Bill

Bill was of course referring to his possible transfer to an officer candidate school. In July of 1941 a number of officer candidate schools were started to help provide the officers needed for the rapidly expanding army. There was the Infantry School at Fort Benning, Georgia, an Air Corps School, Field Artillery and many others. Candidates were sought from among qualified enlisted men already in the army. Commanders were to encourage their best men to apply. While intelligence was an obvious prerequisite, leadership ability was the single most important quality needed.

OCS courses lasted three months. Thus, a pool of accepted applicants was necessary to fill the beginning classes and keep turning out brand new second lieutenants. A commander's desire to keep his best enlisted men, rather than lose them to a school, was natural and had to be guarded against by War Department detectives. After acceptance, while waiting for actual assignment and transfer to a class, it was natural to worry that something might happen to interfere with that assignment.

Bill was keeping up with the war news too. His reference to "7 ships sunk over the weekend" was correct. In its Monday, January 26, 1942 "The War Summarized" column, the *New York Times* reported that

> United States naval forces struck a severe blow over the week-end at the Japanese... The Navy Department at Washington announced that United States cruisers and destroyers in the strait of Macassar had sunk five enemy transports and probably another one, in addition to two reported Saturday.[1]

The Strait of Macassar is between Borneo and Celebes in the Pacific Ocean. In January 1942 the United States and the Dutch military forces fought, unsuccessfully, against Japanese landings and the occupation of Borneo. There was a lot of war left to fight.

But there was good news too. Bill's sister Dorothy gave birth to her first child, a son, Donald Bolenske.

Feb. 1, 1942

Dear Dor,

Your card arrived yesterday. I didn't know that you were expecting your baby so soon. Or maybe it isn't so soon at that. It seems only a couple of months since I was home but it has been all of four months. I hope that both you and the baby are well.

This makes me an uncle three times over. Between you and Jean, you are certainly making me feel old. Wish I could get married and have a few kids of my own, but I suppose I'll have to wait until we get this mess settled.

Write when you feel like it and let me know how you and Don and the baby are.

Bill

---

1   Copyright 1944 by The New York Times Company. Reprinted by permission.

Feb. 3, 1942

Dear Mom,

Will you send me my trumpet? Send it prepaid and take the amt. out of my allotment. Also send my mutes. The ones that look like this:

If you can find my trumpet dance music send it too. It's the music written by hand on individual sheets. It should be in that black case I used to use.

Don't make a special trip home to do this. There is no hurry. One of the new recruits is a piano player and we now have a nice service club where there is a piano. I borrowed a horn last Sunday and we had a swell time.

When my horn comes I'll put a shipping tag on it right away and then if we get sent anywhere I can send it easily.

Hope you and Dunc got straightened out on the money. I'm afraid I wasn't much help.

Also had a birth announcement from Dor.

One other thing. You might take two or three dollars of the allotment money and settle my bill with the Dr. in Fromberg. He fixed a headache for me once.

I think I'll have some good news for you in a month or so but I don't want to spoil it by telling you now, so keep your fingers crossed for me anyway.

Love,
Bill

Feb. 21, 1942

Dear Mom,

Your letter and package both arrived. Thanks for the candy. It was very good. The music is just what I wanted. Guess the trumpet will be along any day now. We're not at the fort anymore but I think that I will be able to carry the horn all right.

We've been stationed near Seattle on guard duty
(don't tell anyone where we are—it's supposed to be a
military secret). My new address and I think it is
permanent is as follows:

Pvt. Wm A. Rogers (A.S.N. 39600334)
Co. C 15th Infantry
A.P.O. Tacoma, Washington

At army post office no. 3 in Tacoma the army takes
over our mail and delivers it wherever we are.

Your plan to train for a defense job is an excellent
one. However, I think you are right about not going to
Indiana. I presume that Donnie has gone by now. Don't
worry about him. I think that he has pretty good sense.

Were you able to get Edna's address? If you could get
it from her Aunt, Mrs. Flatmo, I would appreciate it muchly.

Hope you get your vacation. I think that you'll have a
lot of fun visiting Wynn.

No Chris didn't come to see me. He wrote that he was
coming but never showed up, so I wrote to him. Now that
I've moved I doubt that I'll get to see him.

Did you get the photo album I sent you?

Can't understand why the allotment money hasn't
arrived. You are supposed to get it on or about the 4th of
each month.

> Love,
> Bill

On February 19 the President signed Executive Order 9066.
The Order empowered the Secretary of War to define "military areas" and to remove from them such persons as he saw
fit. On February 23 the Japanese submarine I-17 shelled Santa
Barbara, California. In March all Japanese-Americans on the
West Coast were forcibly removed and settled in relocation
camps.

March 18, 1942

Dear Mom,

I'm glad you had such a good time in Texas. I was
sure you would. From your description the climate is a lot
like this part of Washington. It's anything but flat here
tho. Some of the city streets are so steep that the
sidewalks have steps.

Thanks for sending the pics. I'm returning them as I
have no place to put them. Jean looks a little thin. Had a
letter from her, she is certainly pleased with her new
piano. Why don't you send her all my sheet music and
there is a book of piano accompaniment that she might
like. It is the one with the stiff cover and sort of spiral
binding.

Glad that Tom has moved. Did he move all the stock
and equipment? I wish you would sell that farm so you
could forget about it.

Yes I got the tpt [trumpet]. It came while I was in
Seattle on guard duty. I've complained about the money.
They have deducted $15 a month for two months and it
should have been sent to you.

We were on guard at Boeing in Seattle. While we
were there I got to ride in a B-17 bomber. Don't
remember whether I told you or not. It was a swell ride.
We were up for 45 minutes.

I haven't seen Chris. He writes once in a while but he
never comes out and I can't get in there.

Guess that's all for now.

Love, Bill

April 1, 1942

Dear Mom,

What a surprise. So the ranch has finally been sold?
I'm glad. It sounds as though you had made a pretty good
deal.

I'm going to have just as big a surprise for you, soon
now I hope.

Has my allotment money ever arrived? You should
have $45.00 now. I checked on it at this end and it's

alright. They said just to be patient that sometimes they were delayed.

I thought that you would like Texas. Hope you can go back to stay. Jean is planning on an awfully long visit. Where is she going to stay?

Sorry but there won't be any more furloughs as far as I know. We can only get away from the fort for eight hrs. at a time.

Jean writes to me very often. She and the family are well and happy. Al is working for the Carbaloy Co. an accountant or something.

The pics are very good, but what in thunder were you doing in front of the colored men's service club? Wynn and Pearl look good. She writes to me once in a great while.

Thank you for the swell cookies. When I got to my bunk I had acquired about 30 friends who were very helpful about cutting the string, unwrapping the paper and incidentally, eating the cookies.

Mrs. Buckley sent me a spice cake. She didn't know that it was my birthday but the cake arrived right on the twenty-ninth.

Had a letter from Donnie. He is well pleased with the change he has made. He has a nice room and gets good hot meals at the house next door.

Frank sent me two dollars for my birthday. Nice of him.

I'm sending you my little photo albums and some negatives in little tin cans. Stick them away some where for me.

We just had dinner, very good too. Chicken soup, meat loaf, mashed potatoes with brown gravy, green salad and fruit salad.

My friend Ray Allen has been promoted to acting communications sergeant. That means that he does the work without the rating or the pay. He'll get them soon.

They tried to make me "chief bugler" of the regiment but I turned it down. Have a prospect of something much better.

Captain Billings has been promoted and is now in regimental headquarters so we have a new Co. commdr.

His name is Wayne R. Hill. He's only a first lieut. but he seems to know his stuff.

Don't forget to get me Edna's address if you can.

I go to the show several times a week. There isn't much else to do.

Have to go to bugle school now. Bye.

> Love,
> Bill

April 11, 1942

Dear Mom,

Haven't much to say, but I have the time to write, so I'll do it just to let you know that I'm still alright.

I found out why the money didn't get to you. The personnel office had put the wrong address on the papers. It's being straightened out now.

The cigarettes came a few days after the cookies. Thank you very much. I sent the big album ages ago. Can't understand why you haven't gotten it, if that's the one you mean. I'm going to send the little ones to Jean, but I don't think I mentioned that when I wrote to you.

Thanks exceedingly for Edna's address. I didn't think that Mrs. Flatmo would remember me. She only saw me once. She was an awfully nice person.

Had a letter from Alvina. She's in San Francisco. Married to Eddie Meridith. My heart is broken. Never again shall I trust a woman. Except maybe Bettie or Edna or my girl in Kelso Wash. Or, probably any other one that asks me to.

Don't send any more stamps. My mail goes free now. Goody, goody.

My friend Ray Allen has been promoted and is now the communication Sergeant, which makes him my immediate boss, which is fine.

Guess that is all for now Mom. Not much, but it's a darned sight prompter than my letters usually are.

> Love,
> Bill

IV
OCS

On April 16, 1942, "Pvt 1 cl WILLIAM A. ROGERS, 39600334, Co C, 15th Inf." was ordered, along with sixteen other enlisted men, "trfd <u>in gr</u> to Inf Officer Candidate School, Class No 37, Ft. Benning, Ga.... not later than Apr. 22, for duty...."

The same day, and in keeping with another "Officer Candidate Schools" War Department directive, Bill and the other Fort Lewis "Pvt 1 cl" candidates designated to travel with him <u>in gr</u>, were promoted to Corporal. OCS kept them all busy.

April 27, 1942

Dear Mom,

Arrived at Benning late Tuesday nite. Since then I have been on the go continuously. We have classes for eight hours a day and then have to study nearly four hours. It isn't too hard, just lots of it.

Haven't written to Bettie yet, so you can see that I've really been busy.

The instructors here are excellent. If they weren't we wouldn't be able to grasp the amount of work that is put before us.

I am rapidly becoming friends with a really fine fellow. His name is Gerhard Rehder, and he was, of all things, a professor of History at Bowdoin College in Maine, before joining the army.

It's noon now. Had to quit writing to go to class.

Nothing much to say. Had a nice trip down. It's hot here and all that. Just wanted to give you my new address. Incidentally, when you get the first allotment check, keep it in return for the $15.00 I got from you. After that, cash the checks and send me a money order for them. We have a lot of expenses here that we didn't

39

have at Ft. Lewis. That's why I made out an allotment. I
expected tho that by the time I left for Benning that
several checks would have piled up and so I would have
a cash reserve, but the personnel office got the address
mixed up.

>   Love,
>   Bill

"I was actually writing a letter to you when one of the fellows snapped
this photo."

Bill enthusiastically attacked his OCS studies, and ex-
celled. Gerhard Rehder, now a retired history professor, is
convinced he would not have graduated from OCS without
Bill's personal tutelage. In an April 1990 letter Gerhard recalled
his impression of Bill during their "Benning" days: "an independent spirit, somewhat unorthodox, a wry sense of humor,
bright, witty...."
While Bill, Gerhard, and their classmates worked and
studied hard, civilians were about to undergo the first of their

many hardships, rationing. On May 4, 1942, Americans registered with their local boards and received War Ration Book Number One, the "sugar book." Before long coffee, meat, gas, and tires were rationed.

Classmate Gerhard Rehder

(SO #82, Hq 3d Inf Div, cs, 4/16/42) Cont'd)

4. Pursuant to authority contained in WD ltr, AG 352 (3-5-42) MT A M; dated Mar 8, 1942, subject: "Officer Candidate School, The Infantry School, Class No 37, and under the provisions of Cir 48 WD 1942, the following named EM; orgns as indicated, are trfd in gr to Inf Officer Candidate School, Class No 37, Ft Benning, Ga, and WP at the proper time fr this sta to Ft Benning, Ga, reporting upon arrival thereat to the Commandant, Inf Officer Candidate School, Class No 37, not later than Apr 22, 1942 for duty:

       Tech Sgt CHARLES A. ESCH, 6546688, Hq Co, 15th Inf. (In Charge)
       St Sgt WALLACE B. MARTIN, 6576565, AT Co, 15th Inf.
       St Sgt ORVILLE PUCKETT, 6854905, Hq Co, 15th Inf.
       St Sgt LEO C. CRAWFORD, 6862187, Co A, 15th Inf.
       St Sgt CARVEL BINGHAM, 6559891, Hq Co, 15th Inf.
       Sgt LEROY G. BALKWELL, 6571692, Co F, 15th Inf.
       Sgt CURTIS F. LIVINGSTON, 6933193, Hq Det 1st Bn, 15th Inf.
       Sgt PAUL J. DURAND, 6930632, Co C, 15th Inf.
       Sgt ARNOLD L. BJORKLUND, 39375753, Co B, 15th Inf.
       Sgt VIRGIL G. BROWN, 6589024, Co M, 15th Inf.
       Corp JACK R. ISAACS, 17002430, Co I, 15th Inf.
       Corp CHARLES H. KESSE, 37006591, Serv Co, 15th Inf.
Pvt 1 cl Specl 5cl CHESTER L. TANNEHIL, Band, 15th Inf.
Pvt 1 cl Specl 5cl WILLIAM P. SORNOFF, 36033955, Serv Co, 15th Inf.
       Pvt 1 cl LEO MILLER, 39379032, Band, 15th Inf.
       Pvt 1 cl WILLIAM A. ROGERS, 39600334, Co C, 15th Inf.
       Pvt 1 cl KENNETH A. PHELEY, 39081348, Hq Co, 15th Inf.

Under the provisions of Cir 48 WD 1942, as amended by teletype, quoted in ltr, this Hq, 352 (AG-EM), dated Apr 6, 1942, subject: "Officer Candidate Schools", Pvts 1 cl Specl 5th cl TANNEHIL and SORNOFF and Pvts 1 cl MILLER, ROGERS, and PHELEY will be promoted to the 5th Grade effective two days prior to departure.

The QMC will furnish the necessary rail transportation.

It being impracticable for the govt to furnish rations in kind; the QM will furnish meals for seventeen (17) men under the provisions of par 2, AR 30-2215, for such meals as the length of the journey may require at a rate not to exceed $0.75 per meal or not to exceed $1.00 per meal per man when meals are taken in the dining car.

TDN and payment when made is chargeable to procurement authority FD 1401 P 7-06 A 0410-2.

The above named EM will take with them such individual clothing as is authorized in TBA. Individual equipment taken will consist of two barracks bags, identification tags with tape, toilet set and towels, only.

5. So much of par 5, SO 79, this Hq, cs, pertaining to the asgmt of FA Off, as reads " the VOCG of Mar 25, 1942", is amended to read "the VOCG of Mar 24, 1942.

XXX   XXX   XXX

By command of Major General ANDERSON:

OFFICIAL:

LAWTON BUTLER,
Lt. Col., A.G.D.,
Adjutant General.

WALTER E. LAUER;
Colonel, G.S.C.,
Chief of Staff.

TEMPORARY WARRANT
Sec I, Cir 122,
War Dept., June 23, 1941.

Army of the United States

To all who shall see these presents, greeting:

Know ye, *that reposing special trust and confidence in the fidelity and abilities* of ___Private First Class WILLIAM A. ROGERS, 39600334,___ *, I do hereby appoint him* ___Corporal (Temp), Company "C", 15th Infantry___ , ARMY OF THE UNITED STATES, *to rank as such from the* ___Sixteenth___ *day of* ___April___ *one thousand nine hundred and* ___Forty Two___ *He is therefore carefully and diligently to discharge the duty of* † ___Corporal___ *by doing and performing all manner of things thereunto belonging. And I do strictly charge and require all Noncommissioned Officers and Soldiers under his command to be obedient to his orders as* ___Corporal___ *And he is to observe and follow such orders and directions from time to time, as he shall receive from his Superior Officers and Noncommissioned Officers set over him, according to the rules and discipline of War.*

Given under my hand at ___Fort Lewis, Washington___ *this* ___Sixteenth___ *day of* ___April___ *in the year of our Lord one thousand nine hundred and* ___Forty Two___

THOS. H. MONROE
Colonel, 15th Infantry

W. D., A. G. O. Form No. 58
March 29, 1930

May 10, 1942

Dear Mom,

Thanks for the money. It came at an opportune time. Yes, that was the correct amount. There should be one each month until I graduate, at which time the allotment automatically ends.

We had almost the whole weekend free this week. It seemed too good to be true. Bought a pair of swimming trunks and went to an outdoor pool in Columbus. A few more trips like that and I'll have a glorious tan.

I like the climate here in Georgia. It is hot during the day but is usually cool enough at night to make sleeping comfortable. Much nicer than winter in Washington. We wear khakis all the time. The climate is about all I like about this state however. The fort, in typical army style, is built out in the country and the only towns within striking distance are small. This results in the usual proportion of 14 soldiers for every civilian on the streets.

Bill at Ft. Benning

I have been chosen to act as platoon commander for next week. As there are fifty men in a platoon and only twelve or thirteen of them can hold this position, I feel that I have been honored more than a little.

I made a score of about 99 on the 'graded test' on map reading, and did almost as well on the M-1 rifle G.T. Last Monday <u>night</u>, as part of our map training, we were dumped out of trucks in the middle of the wilderness, given a regular map of the area and an aerial photograph, on which was a little mark indicating where we then were, and another mark indicating the assembly point. We had to choose our own path and trails and wind up at the assembly point about three miles away. This was fairly easy, although it had to be done in the dark. Then Tuesday <u>night</u> we were again dumped out, with nothing but compasses, and given a set course to follow for a definite distance. The course I had to follow was this. Walk 740 yards on an azimuth of 243 degrees, 960 yds on an azimuth of 43 degrees and 1080 yds on an azimuth of 51 degrees. This direction led thru dense woods and swamps, bare hills and some bushy valleys, but we (a party of four) came within fifty yards of our destination, which is pretty good. Incidentally, azimuth is simply the army's way of saying North East, or South West by South.

We heard yesterday that the army officials were trying to get President Roosevelt to come down to Benning for the 4th of July. If he does, they will graduate a lot of us a week or two early so that he can hand us our diplomas. Won't that be a thrill?

We should be good officers after we finish this course. We certainly get the finest training of army officer's schools in the world. Even the British O.S. doesn't compare with this one.

Betty seemed pleased, but not over enthusiastic about my promotion. When we finish the course we are supposed to be able to get a 10 day furlough. If I do, I'm going to Detroit and ask her to marry me. If she can't make up her mind by then, I guess I'll start looking for another girl.

Guess that's all for now Mom. Give my regards to everyone.

> Love,
> Bill

On May 15 gasoline was rationed. Americans holding an "A" card were limited to only three gallons a week! By the end of 1942 ten items were being rationed.

Bill's enthusiasm for his classwork wasn't dampened by rationing or anything else.

May 24, 1942

Dear Mom,

This course gets better as it goes on. We're learning so many new things that we never get bored. That was the biggest fault with "line duty" as an enlisted man you know. I'm doing very well so far. We've had graded tests on four subjects now and I have done very well on them. One of them was perfect.

This coming week we will study the bayonet, grenade and Browning Automatic Rifle. After one week's study we are expected to know them thoroughly, so you can see how intense this course is. The enlisted men spend several months covering these weapons.

The food here is terrible but I've been working hard and haven't lost any weight so I guess it is good for you. No, don't send me anything. By the time packages get to us they are usually mauled and battered out of shape.

Had a letter from Donnie yesterday. He is all right. He and Dad are moving to the place where they board.

I read about Mr. Markuson's death. Gene Grossen sent me a copy of the Fromberg Herald. The pictures are swell, but I've got to send them back as I have no place to keep them. You're looking well. After I get my commission I will have my picture taken in my new uniform and send it to you.

Yes I have to buy my own clothes now and when I graduate I have to buy a whole set of officer's clothes. The Govt. gives us $150 for this but it isn't enough. I think I'll sell my trumpet. I never have time to play it anymore anyway. Send the allotment money as fast as it arrives. I'll need it.

Went flying today. In a little Taylor Craft. A friend of mine here is a pilot. We were up half an hour. If I am not sent to combat duty as soon as I graduate I think that I will learn to fly. It isn't difficult, and not nearly as expensive as I thought.

I'm not sure what I will do after the war. Business of some kind I presume. We are only commissioned as Reserve Lt's. and when the war is over we are discharged. I'd still like to start that photographic supply store, and I think that after the war I'll have money enough.

No thanks, I don't think I'd care for Gladys or any other girl. If I can't have Bettie, I guess I'll do without. I don't doubt that she'll marry me eventually, but I'll probably have to get a few silly notions out of her head first.

Have you heard from Jean? I wrote to her about my good fortune but she hasn't answered. The Emersons look well in the photograph, but they have changed a lot since I last saw them. Aren't any of the boys in uniform?

That's all for now.

Love,
Bill

June 4, 1942

Dear Mom,

Glad, as always, to hear from you. Had a letter from Dad, and Don is alright. I'm worried about Jean. I've written her two or three times and she hasn't answered. Haven't heard from her since I came to Benning and that's over six weeks ago. She used to write every week.

Margaret Lyons sent me a card so I wrote to her. I think she's awfully nice. Had a date with her once you know. She was sure full of fun.

We had a class picture taken. I bought two copies. One for you and one for Bettie. I'll send you your copy tonight I think, if not, then this Saturday.

Please send my allotment money as soon as you receive it. And will you make a note of the month for which the check is being paid (that is if it says on the check)? I should have two coming and I don't think that you will get more than one. If that is so I'll try to collect at this end.

Candidate Bill Rogers (seated center)

We're studying the mortars now. They are an awfully good weapon. They will throw a high explosive shell nearly a mile and hit a small target.

I think that when I have graduated that we will be given ten day furloughs. If we do I am going to Detroit to see Bettie. I'll stop at La Porte and see Dad and Don, and while I'm in Detroit I'll see Jean and Frank. May get married if Bettie can make up her mind. I don't suppose she will.

I'm figuring on selling my trumpet, and I wrote to Uncle Don asking him to lend me a hundred dollars. I'll be able to pay it back easily after I am commissioned.

It rained buckets of water on us for a few minutes yesterday while we were sitting in the stands watching a "motor reconnaissance" demonstration. We all got soaking wet, but we were perfectly dry again in an hour.

I'm going into Columbus tonight to get a hair cut and price some officers uniforms. We have to order them pretty soon. Won't I look slick in custom made clothes and a Sam Brown Belt? I'll send you a picture.

We have some men here from Fort Leonard Wood. Guess Chris could have gone to a worse place but none of the men here know of one. Glad Jack likes the Navy. I doubt very much that he is at sea yet. Sailors have to take a long course at a naval training base before they are assigned to a ship.

Went to a show last night (soldier show) and they had one of those "community sings" where the words are thrown on screen and the audience all sing. One of the songs they had divided up into parts for men, and girls alone and when they said "girls only" you should have heard the soldiers roar. Then they all began to sing falsetto.

Time to fall out again so this is all for now. Write soon.

Yes I worry when I don't get letters. What with gas and food rationing, and possible compulsory defense labor, I never know for sure what is happening to anyone until I hear from them.

Love,
Bill

June 30, 1942

Dear Mom,

Pleased as usual to get your letter. Don't wait so long next time. I'm always afraid that something might have happened to you. Don't know what could, guess I'm just a worrier.

I've written Edna and had an answer, and have written to her again in Red Lodge. My first letter caught her just before she left Sitka.

We only have eighteen days left and then I'm a Second Lieutenant. You are right about the pay, we will get $150 a month. Officers in the Paratroops get an extra hundred a month.

This letter was interrupted. It is now Wednesday the 1st. Friday, the men who are not going to be commissioned are dropped from the class. We don't know exactly who they are but we have a good idea. Tough luck for them, but it would be a darn sight tougher to give them fifty men to lead into combat.

You'll have to wait awhile for the rest of this letter. The food here is terrible, so I'm going down to the service club and get some soup and a salad.

Don't quite know how it happened but it is now Saturday the 4th of July. We had a full day today and I'm pretty tired. I sold my trumpet. Now I'll have plenty of money for my furlough, if I get one.

Two weeks from today I'll be a 2nd Lieutenant!!! After I reach my next post I'll have a studio portrait made and send you a copy.

The men who were to be dropped Friday are still here and they are certainly confused. They don't know whether they have made the grade or not.

I've had several letters from Detroit. Jean and Bettie have made some swell plans for my leave. Jean and Al are taking Bettie and I out to Northwood Inn for dinner, and Jean is going to hold an open house, so I'll get to see everyone.

Then Bettie has gotten up a party to go niteclubbing. And we are going to the Army Show of Irving Berlin's. It's in Detroit the week that I'll be there. Bettie has a cousin Dave in the show, so perhaps we'll get backstage.

I may fly north so that I can spend a day with Dad and Donnie. It doesn't cost much more than 1st class pullman and takes only a few hours.

We just finished another week of tactics. They certainly give us elementary stuff. I think I'll be a good tactician if it's as simple as this.

I went riding last Sunday and I'm going again tomorrow. Swimming too if I feel like it. Trouble is that we only get Sundays off and I try to do too much and tire myself out.

. . . . . [torn letter]

July 12, 1942

Dear Mom,

Thanks for the check. I've got plenty of money now, since I sold my horn. Wish you would come to Detroit while I am there. Don't know when I'll get to see you again. I can pay your fare one way and I think Jean and Al will pay the other if you want to go back to Montana. How about it Mom? You're not doing anything right now that can't wait a little while. And don't worry about the money, I've got almost $200. As far as working, you won't have to anymore. As a Lieutenant I'll make enough so that I can give you an allotment high enough to live on. How about it Butch? Meet me in Detroit. I won't get to Detroit until Sunday.

Lots of love,
Bill

On July 16, 1942, Corporal William A. Rogers received an Honorable Discharge from the Army of the United States "by reason of Convenience of the Government to accept appointment as Second Lieutenant and Active Duty in the Army of the United States."

On July 17, 1942, William Andrew Rogers, Gerhard Rehder, and the other successful candidates were informed that the "President has appointed and commissioned you a temporary Second Lieutenant, Army of the United States . . . ." Bill was ordered to report to Camp Wolters, Texas, not later than July 31, 1942. And, as a delay in reporting was authorized as "in int pub serv," he came to Detroit. Ivy couldn't make that visit.

𝕳onorable 𝕯ischarge

from

𝕿he 𝕬rmy of the 𝕬nited 𝕾tates

TO ALL WHOM IT MAY CONCERN:

This is to Certify, That* _____ WILLIAM A. ROGERS _____

† _39600334, Corporal, Fourth Company, Third Student Training Regiment_

THE ARMY OF THE UNITED STATES, as a TESTIMONIAL OF HONEST AND FAITHFUL SERVICE, is hereby HONORABLY DISCHARGED from the military service of the UNITED STATES by reason of ‡ ___Convenience of the__ Government to accept appointment as Second Lieutenant and Active Duty in the Army of the United States, Section X, AR 615-360.

Said _____ WILLIAM A. ROGERS _____ was born

in _____Detroit_____, in the State of _____Michigan_____

When enlisted he was 22 11/12 years of age and by occupation a ___Farmer___

He had _Blue_ eyes, _Brown_ hair, _Fair_ complexion, and

was ___5___ feet ___5___ inches in height.

Given under my hand at _____Fort Benning, Georgia_____ this

_16th_ day of _____July_____, one thousand nine hundred and _forty-two_

R. N. Sord

_____R. H. LORD,_____
Colonel, Infantry,

                                                     Commanding.

See A R 345-470.
*Insert name; as, "John J. Doe."
† Insert Army serial number, grade, company, regiment, or arm or service; as "1620302"; "Corporal, Company A, 1st Infantry"; "Sergeant, Quartermaster Corps."
‡ If discharged prior to expiration of service, give number, date, and source of order or full description of authority therefor.   16—10565

W. D., A. G. O. Form No. 55
April 30, 1941

HEADQUARTERS THIRTY-SIXTH DIVISION
APO #36 - Dilworth, North Carolina

August 10, 1942

SPECIAL ORDERS

NO.   197   E X T R A C T

X   X   X

9. The following named officers, having reported at this Headquarters,
this date in compliance with paragraph 1, Special Orders No. 186, Headquarters
Infantry Replacement Training Center, Camp Wolters, Texas, dated August 1, 1942,
are assigned to duty with the units shown:

141ST INFANTRY

2nd Lt ROBERT L. DAVEY, O-1288017, Inf-AUS
2nd Lt PARKHURST C. HOUGH, O-1288056, Inf-AUS
2nd Lt WALLACE B. MARTIN, O-1288089, Inf-AUS
2nd Lt REYNOIDS D. RODGERS, O-1288125, Inf-AUS

142ND INFANTRY

2nd Lt RALPH D. KNOX, O-1288073, Inf-AUS
2nd Lt THEODORE J. NYKIEL, O-1288103, Inf-AUS
2nd Lt WILLIAM A. ROGERS, O-1288126, Inf-AUS

143RD INFANTRY

2nd Lt LOUIS H. DeARMAS, O-1288020, Inf-AUS
2nd Lt JAMES D. O'NEILL, O-1288107, Inf-AUS

X   X   X

By command of Major General WALKER:

JOHN D. FORSYTHE,
Colonel, General Staff Corps,
Chief of Staff.

OFFICIAL:

MARVIN D. STEEN,
Lt Col, Adjutant General's Department,
Adjutant General.

DISTRIBUTION "E"

August 2, 1942

Dear Mom,

Wanted to let you know that I was all right. I've got
my commission and am a part of the army again.

Had a marvelous time while I was in Detroit, except
that Bettie wouldn't marry me and I decided that I had
been a 'damn fool' long enough and told her so. Maybe
I'll look her up after the war—maybe not.

Jean's kids are nice. Seem to be pretty smart for their
ages. Al was swell to me. Let me use his car all the time I
was there.

Saw Frank and Mary. He's getting old. They were very
nice.

By the way, don't write to me here. I'm leaving for a
new post in a few days. When I have been definitely
assigned somewhere, I'll send you my address. Don't
worry if you don't hear from me for awhile, it may be
sometime before I have my definite address.

Love,
Bill

Saw Frank

and Mary

August 8, 1942

Dear Mom,

Just a line to let you know my new address. Will have more complete one later.

Had a nice, uneventful trip to Texas. Liked my new station very much but only stayed there four days, then received orders to proceed to this new station. Traveled by car with a friend of mine.

Will write more later, when I know what I am going to do.

Love,
Bill

The Infantry School
United States Army

***

This is to Certify that

Corporal William Andrew Rogers

has successfully completed the

Officer Candidates Course

given during the period

April 21, 1942 to July 19, 1942

and has been recommended for a Commission
as Second Lieutenant in the Army of the
United States

For the Commandant

H. B. Wheeler

Colonel of Infantry
Secretary

RESTRICTED

SYMBOLS: WP - Will proceed
PAC - Pursuant to authority contained in
UP - Under provisions of
TDN - Travel directed is necessary in the military service
TPA - If travel is performed by privately owned automobile for permanent change of station only, DS authorized par 1g, AR 605-180.

HEADQUARTERS THE INFANTRY SCHOOL

SPECIAL ORDERS)   Fort Benning, Ga.
          :   17, July, 1942.
NO....173.....)

EXTRACT

x   x   x

2. PAC par 2, Ltr, Hq R&S Comd, AGF, R&SC 210.31-Inf Sch-GNRSP, subject; "Assignment of OCS No. 36", dated 8 July 1942, the following 2nd Lt AUS, are placed on temp duty with IRTC, Cp Wolters, Tex prior to permanent asgmt to 102d Inf Div, Cp Maxey, Tex. WP sd fr Ft Benning, Ga to Cp Wolters Tex reporting upon arrival to CG, IRTC for duty. UP AR 605-115 and PAC pr 12c, WD Cir 126, 1942, a delay in obeying asgmt orders is auth, being considered in int pub serv, provided ea O reports to CG, IRTC, Cp Wolters, Tex for duty with Inf NOT later than July 31, 1942. TPA. TDN. FD 34 P 434-02, 03 A 0425-23.   FD 31 431-02,03 A 0425-23.

x   x   x

ROGERS, WILLIAM A., 01288128

x   x   x

By command of Brigadier General ALLEN:

                                              THORNTON CHASE,
                                              Colonel, A.G.D.,
                                              Adjutant General.

OFFICIAL:

          (S/T) THORNTON CHASE,
                Colonel, A.G.D.,
                Adjutant General.

A TRUE COPY:

                McRAE W. HILL
                2nd Lt., Infantry
                Acting Adjutant.

V
The "Texas" Division

On August 10, 1942, Bill reported for duty with the 36th Division Headquarters, then located in Dilworth, North Carolina. The 36th Division was originally the Texas National Guard. The Texans had been called into the Federal Service on November 25, 1940, and since their induction they had been supplemented by regular army replacements. The Division insignia is a sky blue arrowhead with a large "T" (for Texas) superimposed upon it. The insignia is worn as a shoulder patch and the Division, or its men, are often referred to as "T-Patchers."

When Bill joined the 36th Division, like all "triangular" U.S. Army Infantry Divisions, it consisted of three regiments. In this case, the 141st, 142nd, and the 143rd. Bill was assigned to the 142nd Regiment. Each regiment is made up of three battalions, 1st, 2nd, and 3rd.

A battalion is the basic fighting unit of the infantry. It consists of battalion headquarters, that is the battalion commander and his staff, a headquarters company, three rifle companies, and a heavy weapons company. On August 12, 1942, by special order no. 178, the 142nd Infantry, at that time near Hoffman, N.C., assigned Bill to "Hq Company 2nd Bn."

The rifle and heavy weapons companies are designated by letters. Bill's 2nd Battalion had "E," "F," "G," and "H" Companies. First Battalion has Companies "A" through "D" while 3rd has "I," "K," "L," and "M" ("J" is not used). Companies are further divided into platoons and platoons into squads. Bill was assigned to command the anti-tank platoon of Headquarters Company—but he tells it best. He approached this new job with his typical energy and enthusiasm.

HEADQUARTERS 142ND INFANTRY   SDH/rwm

                                        Near Hoffman, N. C.
                                        August 12, 1942

SPECIAL ORDER:

NO   178:

    1. The following named officers, having reported to 142nd Infantry
for duty, are assigned as follows:

2nd Lt.   THEODORE J. NYKIEL   O-1288103   Company I
2nd Lt.   WILLIAM A. ROGERS   O-1288126   Hq Company 2nd Bn
2nd Lt.   RALPH D. KNOX   O-1288073   Company B

    2. 2nd Lt. JOHN E. HAALAND, O-1288046, Inf., is relieved from assign-
ment and duty with Company I and is assigned to Headquarters Company 3rd
Bn, for duty.

    3. The following named Enlisted Men are transferred to Medical Detac-
ment from Cannon Company:

        Pvt.   Roger H. Kauffman   33201478
        Pvt.   Edward J. McGiff   33201559
        Pvt.   James C. Mekan   33316084

    4. Cpl. Richard H. Faulkner, 38026258, Hq Company 1st Bn, is promoted
to the grade of Staff Sergeant.

                            By order of Colonel SKINNER:

                                        Shirly D. Helns
                                        1st Lt, 142nd Infantry
                                        Asst. Adj.

OFFICIAL: DISTRIBUTION:
                                    1 Copy - each Officer concerned
        Shirly D. Helns   1 Copy - to each 201 file concerned
   1st Lt, 142nd Infantry   2 Copies - to each Unit concerned
        Asst. Adj.   1 Copy - Hq 142nd Infantry
                                    1 Copy - C.G., 36th Division
                                    1 Copy - File

August 23, 1942

Dear Mom,

Have been looking for a letter from you but guess I have been moving too fast for it to catch up with me. First Camp Wolters, Texas—then Wadesboro, North Carolina and now Massachusetts. Doubt that I will be here very long.

I'm very pleased with my first assignment. I have the anti-tank platoon of Headquarters Co of the 2nd Battalion of the 142 Infantry, I have forty men, four 37 millimeter anti-tank guns and nine "jeeps" in my platoon.

The officers in this outfit are swell. The Bn. Commander's name is Col. Goddard. We have a Catholic Chaplain named Quinn, whom every one calls the "parson." I have a new friend. He's a brand new "Fort Benning" 2nd Lt. who has the communications section of Bn. Hq. Co. His name is Robert Cromwell. He used to be on the stage in New York and tells the most fascinating stories about theater people.

My company commander's name is Lt. Beasley. He's a good man. Just about my age and a recent bridegroom. Incidentally, the 36th Division is the Texas National Guard.

I'm going to have an allotment of $50 a month made out to you. This is for your own use. If you don't need it, buy some bonds. If you want to use the money to get your debts straightened up, go ahead.

Think that I'll take out two $5,000 insurance policies. One for you and one for Dad. Haven't decided for sure yet. I don't like insurance. It seems too much like asking for a hole in the head.

Write soon and let me know how you are.

Love,
Bill

When he joined 2nd Battalion, Bill also acquired a nickname: "Buck," or sometimes "Little Buck" Rogers, after the then popular movie hero "Buck Rogers" played by actor Buster Crabbe. He was good at his work.

Writing to Ivy in 1945, former Corporal Charles W. Stimson Jr. said:

> 'Little Buck' as he was known to us, tho I believe you called him 'Bill,' was one of the best liked officers I have ever known. . . . Buck was anti-tank platoon leader of our company for many months. He served that position fully. . . .

In December 1990 former anti-tank platoon Sergeant G.G. McCullough still remembered Bill: "He was about 5 ft 7 in tall. About 130 lbs. Slim, trim and neat. He didn't like any foolish tricks."

As an officer it is possible to be well liked and still get the job done. Bill's friend, former actor Bob Cromwell, in a May 1944 letter to Ivy, recalled that "Bill worked hard as an officer—he was a strict disciplinarian—he demanded and got discipline out of his men."

Bob Cromwell

Wood Jenkins

An OCS classmate and fellow 2nd Battalion officer, (former Lieutenant) Wood R. Jenkins, in September 1990 remembered that

> "Bill was a good officer and his men liked him . . . you could always tell when he was around because he got things moving."

Bill's superior officers felt he was doing a good job too.

Lieutenant Colonel (Retired) Carthell N. "Red" Morgan remembers Lt. Rogers. Red Morgan had been one of the Texas National Guardsmen inducted into the Federal Service in 1940. He was a 2nd Battalion staff officer when Bill joined the outfit. Recalling Bill in a May 1990 letter he said:

"Red" Morgan

It was my privilege to be associated with this fine young officer. You probably already know that he was the commanding officer of the anti-tank platoon of the 2nd Bn 142 Inf. He was familiarly known as "Buck" to the officers of the battalion.

Lt. Rogers was brave, competent, resourceful, dependable and ready to assume any responsibility assigned to him. He had a keen sense of humor and kept that sense of humor even under the most trying circumstances. He was the kind of officer that commanding officers want to have around.

August 30, 1942

Dear Mom,

It's too late to write much, but I guess I'd better bring you up to date on where I am and what I'm doing.

We left North Carolina and are now at Camp Edwards, Massachusetts. It's about sixty miles from Boston. We are living in tents, but it isn't bad except that it is so dusty.

In a few days we move to another area for some amphibious training. The same thing, I think, that I had in Washington.

I have the anti-tank platoon of Headquarters Co. of the Second Battalion of the 142 Infantry. Guess I told you that before. I have four 37 millimeter anti-tank guns and

nine 1/4 ton trucks (jeeps). I am also the company supply
officer. I like my job very much. It is extremely interesting.
More so than anything else I have ever done.

The officers in this outfit are grand. Especially my Co.
Commander, Lt. Beasley. The Colonel is swell too. At
meals he asks for the coffee, followed at seven second

"I have about
forty men, four
37-millimeter
anti-tank guns
and nine 'jeeps'
in my platoon."

intervals by the sugar and cream. A type of humor that I enjoy muchly.

I spent Sat. nite in Providence, Rhode Island. It's not a bad town, but everything closes up at mid-nite. Not much like Montana.

Since you don't need the money, I am not going to make out an allotment. Instead I will send you a money

---

THE INFANTRY SCHOOL
OFFICE OF THE COMMANDANT

IN REPLY REFER TO:
201- Rogers, William Andrew

FORT BENNING, GEORGIA
July 17, 1942

SUBJECT: Temporary Appointment.

TO: Second Lieutenant William Andrew Rogers   A   -01288126
Infantry, A.U.S.

1. The Secretary of War has directed me to inform you that the President has appointed and commissioned you a temporary Second Lieutenant, Army of the United States, effective this date, in the grade shown in the address above. Your serial number is shown after A above.

2. This commission to continue in force during the pleasure of the President of the United States for the time being, and for the duration of the present emergency and six months thereafter unless sooner terminated.

3. There is inclosed herewith a form for oath of office which you are requested to execute and return. The execution and return of the required oath of office constitute an acceptance of your appointment. No other evidence of acceptance is required. This letter should be retained by you as evidence of your appointment.

By order of the Commandant:

Thornton Chase
COLONEL, A.G.D.
ADJUTANT GENERAL

Inclosure:
Form for Oath of Office.

order from time to time. That way, if I need money at any time I will have it because I will keep enough on hand for emergencies.

I think that we are going to go to California for some desert training. If we do, I think that I will be able to send for you to come and visit me.

Wish I could come back to Montana for a visit. New England isn't bad, but I would like to see some familiar faces again.

By the way, you should address my letters to Lt. Wm A. Rogers, and you call me Lieutenant. Isn't that something?

Love,
Bill

P.S. You sure look good in the pics.

B.

September 6, 1942

Dear Mom,

Yes, your other letters all caught up with me. I think that I received three of them all at once.

I've made a new decision on the allotment. The army wants us to buy bonds and your unit gets credit if you buy them, so I am going to have my allotment made out so that each month they will send you a $50 bond. We will be co-owners. That way, if you ever need the money (after 60 days) you can get it.

This is the 9th. I'm so very short of time that I won't be able to write much. Am enclosing your first bonds.

No time to write to Dorothy. Am enclosing a stamp album for her kid. Will you give it to her?

I'm well and healthy. The army is fitting me for glasses again. Spent this afternoon at the hosp. They dilated my pupils with homatropine and now I can't focus on anything. They will clear up in about three days and I should have my glasses by then.

No time for more now.

Write soon, love,
Bill

There was little time to write just then. The Division was kept very busy with amphibious training in September and October. October's training included a landing exercise on Martha's Vineyard.

On November 8, 1942, in what was called operation "Torch," American forces under General Patton landed near Casablanca in French Morocco. Along with the British, Americans also made landings near Oran and Algiers. While there was still months of fighting and terrible losses ahead, Rommel, who was already in retreat from General Montgomery's October breakout at El Alamein, was getting his own two-front war in North Africa. Bill's old outfit from Fort Lewis, the 3rd Division, was part of General Patton's Army.

Since its induction into Federal Service, the 36th Division had been working very hard to achieve combat readiness. For the past year the Division had the advantage of having Major General Fred L. Walker as its commanding officer. General Walker was a Regular Army career officer assigned to re-place the former National Guard General, Claude V. Birkhead. General Walker knew his business and had the respect of the Division.

Major General Fred L. Walker

The Division's readiness level increased steadily under General Walker's guidance. Knowing they could now be sent overseas any time, General Walker announced a liberal furlough policy. By an order dated November 13, 1942, 2nd Lt. William A. Rogers, along with 28 other officers, was granted a leave of absence. Bill's leave was for 10 days starting November 17. He came to Detroit to spend Thanksgiving with his family.

Detroit Thanksgiving 1942. Ivy, Allen Shaffer, Don Rogers holding Roger Shaffer, "Rog," and Bill Rogers

Al and Jeanne Shaffer

Rog, Ivy, and Donnie met Bill at Jeanne's house in Detroit. There are snapshots of Bill and the family taken in Al and Jeanne's backyard. It is a cool day and all the leaves have fallen. It was the last time they would see each other.

December 14, 1942

Dear Mom,

I couldn't get a typewriter, so you'll have to decipher my scrawl. The allotment has gone thru and will be deducted from this month's pay. You should start receiving it in a month or two. Hope the bonds have started arriving by now. I am having the allotment and the insurance sent to you at Jean's address. I figured that it would be the most permanent address you would have. If you decide to stay permanently in Ypsi, let me know and I'll have everything sent directly to you. The insurance isn't thru yet. It seems that I've waited so long to take out a policy, that I now have to take a physical exam. Incidentally, the insurance doesn't pay off in a lump. Just a monthly installment, so forget the plan I suggested.

Had a letter from Jean. She says that Donnie is working for the Engass Jewelry Co. If I'm not too sleepy when I finish this I will write him.

I'm doing some special work right now. Acting as an umpire for the 636th Tank Destroyer Battalion, while they take a combat efficient test. Interesting work, but it's colder than blazes here and we have to get out at 4:30 am.

We have a new Regimental Commander, a Colonel Forsythe. He seems like a pretty good egg. The Division has been moved from the 6th corps to the 13th corps, so it looks as tho we were going to stay in the States awhile. The 13th corps is charged with the Eastern Sea Coast Defense.

The two Lieutenants from this outfit, Edelin and Hodges, who were so terribly burnt in the Coconut Grove fire, are much better now and have been . . . . [missing text, torn page]

Stayed in Hyannis Saturday nite with Lt. MacIlraith and his wife. They've only been married a few weeks,

but they act as tho they had been married for years. Next
weekend we are going to Coonamessett Club together.
Also a girl from Boston for me.

Bill Beasley, my ex Company Commander was
promoted a short time ago from 1st Lt. to Captain.

I had to appear today as a witness, before a "section
eight" board. A couple of my boys were being examined
to see if they had enough brains to stay in the army. They
are both helplessly dumb, but the board decided that one
of them was bright enough for service, but the other one
is being discharged.

Had a letter from Bettie. She was all kinds of sorry.
But thank-goodness I'm cured. Don't guess I'll ever get
married, I don't think that I'd trust a woman that much,
but I'll have a lot of fun.

Have sent my film off. As soon as it comes back I'll
send you the pictures. There should be some good ones
in that roll.

Am having my teeth worked on. Have had two fillings
and one extraction and have about three fillings to go.
I've gotten over my insane fear of dentists. Matter of pride
I guess. Army officers don't scream in public, and in an
army dental clinic there are about twenty patients being
worked on at the same time in the same room.

Father Quinn just returned from his leave. He's a
grand guy, but it's a good thing that his congregation
back home doesn't know what kind of a life he leads.

I'm wading thru Karl Marx's "Das Kapital." It's very
interesting but awfully deep. Sometimes I get bogged
down and have to go back to the beginning of a chapter
to figure out what he is talking about.

I'm going to quit now and write to Donnie. Take care
of yourself.

Love,
Bill

When Bill's furlough was up Ivy stayed on in Michigan for
a time. She got a job and lived with Mae Reddy, a friend in
Ypsilanti, not far from Detroit.

The Coconut Grove incident with Lts. Edeline and Hodges was a reference to a terrible fire at a popular Boston nightclub. On Saturday night, November 28, 1942, the club was packed with servicemen and civilians when palm tree decorations caught fire. The fire spread fast. Nearly five hundred were trapped and killed when people panicked and tried to push both sides of the club's revolving door at once, jamming it closed while the crowd crushed towards the door.

Bill Rogers and Lt. Beasley at Camp Edwards

"The Parson"
Chaplain
Quinn at right

Evan MacIlraith, now living in California, recalls those Camp Edwards days;

Virginia and I married in November of 1942 and we had a home near Hyannis off base. Bill was a guest of ours many times as we three really enjoyed each other and we shared a lot together... He was a *great* friend and we admired each other's abilities to be outstanding "soldiers" from a civilian background... Bill was small but really tough and afraid of nothing....

Evan MacIlraith

Jean Lyman, the girl Bill mentions in the next letter, was the former college roommate of Virginia MacIlraith.

December 27, 1942

Dear Mom,

Thanks a lot for the present. It's a swell brush and comb—thanks too for the cigarettes you included—they are always welcome.

Haven't received many gifts yet, because of a postal strike in Boston, but received cigarettes and copy of Hemingway's "To Have and Have Not" from Jean. It's a good book but nothing like "For Whom the Bell Tolls."

Dad sent the grandest billfold I've ever seen. It's big, like a book, and you have to carry it inside your coat. It has several compartments in it and a note pad and place for a pen.

Had a very quiet Christmas. We had the day off, but I didn't go anywhere. Read a little bit, and polished my shoes and brass and gave my room a thorough cleaning.

Did I tell you the last time that I wrote? I met a grand girl named Jean Lyman, thru mutual friends, a young married couple, that we know. She actually taught me to Rhumba. Have a date with her next week-end in Boston. She likes to dance and she likes ice-hockey and she's slightly crazy, so we make a pretty good couple.

Donnie hasn't written yet. Wish he would keep in touch with me. Do you hear from him? I've written to him but will write again soon.

Hope you are well and happy. Say hello to Mae for me.

                                        Love,
                                        Bill

On December 30, 1942, General Walker received notice to prepare a regiment for overseas movement at an early date. He selected the 142nd. But, like other overseas movement alerts that fall and winter, it too would be postponed.

Meanwhile, Bill was keeping busy. In addition to his other duties, he successfully completed the 36th Infantry Division junior officer's school on army organization, company administration, courts-martial, mess management, motor maintenance, and communication. General Walker signed his certificate on January 20, 1943.

                                        Jan. 18, 1943
Dear Mom,

I should write oftener, but we are so busy that I just can't make it.

Take the negatives to a camera store (not a drugstore) and show the clerk the negatives that you want prints made from. He will cut them however they need to be cut. Glad you like the snaps. Am enclosing a few more.

Have a horrible cold now but will live thru it. I keep myself greased with Vicks. Remember how I used to like you to rub my chest? Guess it will be long time before that happens again.

Glad that you're feeling good again. If and when those bonds start arriving they should come in a big bunch. I think that I've paid for five of them now. Let me know if you get them. The allotment was mixed up and they didn't start taking it out until this month instead of last so it will probably be awhile before it starts arriving.

Remember that the first one is to pay you the $50.00 that I borrowed and that $30.00 out the next one goes to Dad.

It will make me pretty short. I'll draw about $50.00 a month, but I think that's better.

If I have the cash I always spend it, and I wouldn't write for any unless I really needed it.

Went to Boston, weekend before last, to see my girl and last weekend she came out to Hyannis to see me. Thought for awhile that I was falling in love, but I guess not. She's good looking and lots of fun, but I don't think I'll get serious about her. Too easy to get hurt.

We don't have to pay the 5% tax but my income tax for last year is $84. I'm going to let it ride until after the war.

No, the pic of Dor's baby didn't arrive. Guess it was lost in the mail.

From what you say about the buyer of the ranch, I take it he is making the payment regularly. That's good.

I'd better say good nite now. It's getting late and I think that some sleep would help break this cold.

> Bye now—
> Love,
> Bill

On January 14, 1943, President Roosevelt and Prime Minister Churchill met in Casablanca to discuss the prosecution of the war. Premier Stalin declined an invitation to attend the conference on the grounds that, as Commander-in-Chief, he was personally directing the Russian winter offensive and unable to come.

Roosevelt and Churchill met for ten days. The war was reviewed theater by theater and, ostensibly, Allied military plans for the year 1943 were formulated. On January 26 they issued an Official Communique. Nothing less than the "unconditional surrender" of Germany, Italy, and Japan would be accepted.

January 31, 1943

Dear Mom,

I'll try once more. Here are the snaps, starting with me and working down the table and back up the other side; me, Capt. Rosenberg, Capt. Irvin, Major Hoffman, Colonel Goddard, Lt. Roscoe, Lt. Feltwell, Chaplain Quinn and Lt. Beasley.

I'm sending Dad a letter today. I asked him about the thirty dollars in such a way that I don't think he can refuse. It will take some time for the allotment to start arriving, but I can't understand why the bonds don't get there. I started paying for them in September. You have at least four of them coming.

Will you do me favor? I want you to write to Dorothy and tell her how to find my checker board and chess set and that sticking knife of mine. The one that was made from an army bayonet. Have her send them to me as quickly as she can, as we're never sure just how long we are going to be in any one spot. Thanks.

Don't remember the address of the place I worked so I guess you'll have to take the film to a drug store.

"Starting with me... [far right] me, Capt. Rosenberg, Capt. Irvin, Major Hoffman, Colonel Goddard, Lt. Roscoe, Lt. Feltwell, Chaplain Quinn, and Lt. Beasley."

Ypsilanti might be a good place for me to start a
camera store, if there aren't any there. I'll look into it after
I get this war won.

We've got over a foot of snow here on the level and
it's not all level. Most of our study is indoors now. Not too
cold tho. Glad of that. A little goes a long ways here on
Cape Cod.

My cold is gone now, for which thanks be. I had the
medics mark me "quarters" for a couple of days and
stayed in bed.

The army sure played a dirty trick on me. They said
we were going overseas, so I went to town on what I
thought was my last weekend in the States and threw a
big party. Then the move was called off, and I am left
practically destitute, serves me right. Now maybe I'll stay
home awhile.

Yes I knew Jimmy Danford. Met him at the dances I
used to play. He was a good kid. Don't think that I knew
Laura though.

I stayed up to hear the broadcast about Roosevelt.
You're probably right about them planning the rest of the

Captain Rosenberg, standing, Bill
at right.

war, but I'm afraid that 1943 is too soon to expect the end of it. If the success of the Allies continues at its present pace, it would take a least a year to whip Germany, and then we'll have to have an Army of occupation for a year or two, and we've still got the Japs to clean out. Hope I get in on that. It ought to be a lot of fun. They'll probably do it for the most part with air power, but there should be some work for the Infantry.

I may put in an application for the air corp. I'd like to be a navigator and the physical requirements aren't as strict as they were.

Don't forget to write to Dorothy, will you? And tell her not to wait till next summer to send the things.

Love,
Bill

P.S. Always write your complete return address on the envelope. Sometimes I am where I can't get at my address book and then you don't get any letters for a long time.

B.

February 7, 1943

Dear Mom,

Your letter arrived on a weekend again so I'm able to answer it right away.

I was complimented yesterday by the Bn. Commander. A few weeks ago all the 37 mm gun units in the Division took a written test about the gun. Too technical to try to describe. Anyway, I made the 2nd highest grade of any officer in the Regiment. But what is better still, my platoon scored higher than any other platoon in the Regt. The Colonel is pleased and so am I.

Tomorrow I take my platoon out to the "1000" inch range. We mount 22 caliber rifles inside the barrel of the 37 mm and shoot at miniature silhouette tanks at distance of 1000 inches (87 feet). The targets are moving of course. The nice part of it is that I have the range monopolized for my platoon. I can run the range to suit myself.

Then on Tuesday we go to the Gravity Range. The guns are placed on one hill and a target on wheels runs down a track on the next hill and we fire at it as it descends. We'll use .30 caliber tracer ammunition on that one.

"I made the 2nd highest grade of any officer in the Regiment. But what is better still, my platoon scored higher than any other platoon in the Regt."

Then Wednesday morning we run the "Battle Course." That's a honey! You crawl on your belly for about seventy-five yards, in mud, over logs and thru two wire fences and two trenches, while two machine guns fire tracer ammunition about fifteen inches over your head.

In the afternoon I am putting on a molotov cocktail demonstration for the battalion. I have about fifty quart bottles. You fill them with gasoline and oil and make a wick out of rags. You light the wick and smash the bottle against a tank (we'll use a wrecked car). All in all it should be a pretty interesting week.

Colonel Goddard is back. Don't know whether he is coming back to the 2nd Bn. I haven't had an opportunity to speak to him yet. Wish we'd get him back. I like him.

Thursday night, Lt. Myers, our transportation officer, took me home to dinner and I stayed all night. Felt good to sleep between sheets for a change. He and his wife are both from South Carolina and when they talked fast I couldn't understand a word.

The weather here isn't too bad. The snow is almost all gone. But it has turned cold again and we have a lot of ice.

This letter is competing with a radio and vociferous Lt. whose name is Leaffer, so I guess I had better quit.

Love,

Bill

Colonel Goddard

The War Department had been making constant demands on the 36th Division for the transfer of personnel to new units as cadremen. In frustration, General Walker complained bitterly; "the War Department robs me of my best men!" Probing his memory in November of 1990, Colonel Vincent M. Lockhart, who, in 1943, was one of General Walker's staff officers, thought Colonel Goddard may have been among those transferred to new units.

On February 19, 1943, the entire 36th Division was ordered to move by train to Camp A.P. Hill, Virginia. As an extra problem, the 142nd Combat Team (comprised of the 142nd infantry regiment, a battalion of artillery, and a company of engineers) was ordered to Lowesville, Virginia for mountain training.

February 21, 1943

Dear Mom,

We're moving again. This time we've been ordered to Virginia. Somewhere near Fredricksburg. Will give you my new address as soon as I have one. In the meantime you can write to me here and the Army will forward the mail.

Glad that the allotment got thru all right. Maybe the bonds will start arriving now. Due to some new Army regulation the bond allotments are going to terminate on the 31st of March. I'm not going to renew mine. If we are going to stay in the States I will need the money. You should have about six or seven of them when they finally get there. If you don't need the allotment, you can buy bonds with it in both of our names, then if anything happens to me you won't have any trouble getting them cashed. Dad said that you could have twenty of the thirty dollars. The other ten belongs to Donnie. Would appreciate it if you would send it to him.

Can you let me have a hundred dollars right away? I need it to pay my income tax. I thought that I would be overseas by this time, in which case I could let it go until after the war. But here I am, so Uncle Sam wants his dough.

You can cash that first bond I sent you and you will receive another check for fifty dollars about the fourth of March, so I guess it won't short you too much. If you can't make it, let me know and I'll borrow the money from one of the boys here. Sorry to have to be running to you for money all the time, but I made all my plans figuring that I would be across by this time.

Many thanks to you and Mae for the swell Valentine. You can't miss when you send a soldier cigarettes.

Frank sent me some pictures that were taken while I was on furlough. I haven't any place to keep them so I am sending them on to you. Stick them away in the album.

I wrote to Don as you suggested and imparted a few gems of advice. I don't think that he will have any trouble getting used to military life, the army realizes that the new recruits are still civilians and makes a few concessions to that fact.

Yes I'm still broke, will be for several months, but I can get along all right. Where we're going there won't be much temptation to spend money. It's the bleakest part of the state. It always is, no matter where we go. I'm going to try to get into Washington D.C. at least once. I wouldn't like to have been that close to the Capitol without seeing it.

I should have a pretty good sized nest egg when this thing is over. I'll need it, cause I sure want to start that camera store. Guess I'll hire you to work for me. You'll know more about retail merchandising than I do, by the time I get out of the Army.

I'll try to get some pictures made while I am in Virginia. There should be a photographer in Fredricksburg or Richmond. I should have done that before this, but kept putting if off for some reason.

Didn't have time to put on the Molotov Cocktail demonstration. I had my platoon out on the range, firing. Did I tell you that my platoon made the highest score in the Division anti-tank test? Well they did and I was commended by the Colonel, which made me pretty proud.

These next few days are going to be busy ones, and it's ten thirty so I'd better get to bed.

> All my love,
> Bill

In order to both finance the war and control inflation, Congress had passed new laws and Americans faced new and much higher income and excise taxes. As of November 12, 1942, there was a 5-percent "Victory Tax" increase. Taxes rose sharply in 1943, and were to be paid in advance in quarterly payments beginning March 25. That was to change again. On June 10, 1943, the "Pay-As-You-Go" tax bill was signed. Beginning July 1, 1943, salary and wage earners had at least 20 percent of each paycheck deducted and paid to the government.

On February 27, at 10:00 in the evening, the War Department ordered those elements of the 36th Division not yet moved to Virginia (the 142nd Combat Team had already moved) to remain at Camp Edwards, until given "further orders." Not surprisingly, in his book *From Texas to Rome*, General Walker titled this chapter in the life of the 36th Division: "Order, Counterorder, Disorder."

On March 5 the War Department suspended the 142nd's mountain training at Lowesville, directing that it remain there pending overseas shipment. As Lowesville had no facilities and was otherwise unsuitable, General Walker obtained permission to have the 142nd moved to Camp Hill.

March 6, 1943

Dear Mom,

The check for the hundred dollars arrived a couple of days ago. Thanks very much. That income tax is hard to pay. I think that my tax for next year will be about three hundred dollars.

As I told you, I am dropping my bond allotment, the thirty first of March, but I am going to continue the fifty dollar allotment. Keep it, and as it arrives take out the money that I owe you. If the allotment for February has arrived, I should owe you eighty dollars, The first fifty paid back the fifty that I had borrowed when I was in Detroit, and the next one (February) paid Dad and Donnie and paid twenty dollars on the hundred. After the hundred is all paid, use the money as it arrives for yourself, or if you have no use for it, then buy some more bonds in both our names. When the bonds that I have already paid for finally get there, they should amount to three hundred and fifty dollars. Four hundred with the two twenty-five dollar bonds that I sent last fall. I have a record of the bond allotment being taken out of my pay check, so they will get there eventually. If you should want to check on the bonds and can't get in touch with me, write to the Finance Department, Army of the United States, Washington, giving them my full name and my Army Serial Number (0-1288126).

Your letter arrived just as I was finishing the hardest three days that I have ever put in the army. We are in the Blue Ridge Mountains of Virginia, and it is still winter here. We were out on a three day problem, designed to find out how troops with-out mountain clothing or equipment, could get along in the mountains. I guess they found out! After we got into camp and I got to a stove, it was five minutes before I could even talk. Later I found one of my Sergeants crying as his hands thawed out, and he is no baby. One of the truck drivers in the first Battalion was killed when he overturned his jeep on one of the mountain trails. If you have a good atlas, you may be able to follow our trail on it. We started out at a little town called Jack's Hill. It's about thirty miles from Lynchburg. We climbed the Little Priest Mtn. and crossed the saddle to the Priest Mtn. Then we followed Pinnacle Ridge to its end and dropped down into the valley. We slept the first night on the Priest and the second in the valley of the Tyre River. It would have been fun in the summer. However I'm alive and healthy, so I guess the experience didn't hurt me. I got some good pictures from Pinnacle Ridge.

We're getting ready to move again. Don't know where we're going. The Army is being very mysterious about the whole thing. The rest of the Division was supposed to follow us down here, but their move has been called off, at least temporarily, and they are still Camp Edwards. I doubt that we will ever see them again.

We're back in base camp at Lowesville and I've gotten all my equipment straightened up and my bedding aired and re-rolled. We have no laundry facilities, so I am doing my own. You can imagine how much that pleases me. I have a #10 fruit can and I fill it with soap and water, and boil my clothes, a few at a time on the little stove in my tent.

The three Lieuts. that share my tent have gone to town, so I have the place to myself, which pleases me. I have gotten so I like to be alone. Going to bed as soon as I finish this. It's eleven o'clock and I've only had four hours sleep in the last seventy two.

We actually ran across an old still in the mountains, Just like downtown only not so crowded. These mountains are beautiful. A lot like the Pryors, only there are so many more of them.

Had a short letter from John Clawson. Will write to him as soon as I find time. Had a letter from Uncle Don too. Full of the usual sententious advice. I've written to him several times but he hasn't answered yet.

Can't keep my eyes open another minute, so I'll have
to say good-nite.

Love,
Bill

P.S. Since I wrote this letter our address has been
changed, so I had to tear open the envelope and
address a new one. The address here was 142nd Inf
Combat Team, Amherst, Va. The address that you should
send mail to is as follows: 142nd Infantry. A.P. Hill
Military Reservation, Virginia. We leave for the A.P. Hill
Reservation tomorrow or Monday. It's only about a
hundred miles so we are making the move by truck. It
will be fun if the weather will turn warm.

B.

On March 6, General Walker had received orders to have
those troops at Camp Hill and Camp Edwards ready to have
their property shipped by March 14, 1943. Camp Edwards
personnel were to be ready to be shipped by March 28. Overseas movement was beginning to look certain.

Meanwhile, Ivy had decided to return to her beloved
Montana.

March 15, 1943

Dear Mom,

Nothing much to say. Wanted to write for this same
reason that you wrote to me.

Don wrote that he was working and intended to live
at Mae's. Understand that he is going to finish his
education. That will be fine. I'll help him when I can, if
he needs it.

Glad you're going to Montana as long as that is what
you want. Check up in Montana, the bonds may be
arriving there. If you want the allotment sent to you in
Montana I will have it sent there.

After the war I'll get a good car and we'll see some of
these United States together. From what I have seen of
them in the Army there are a lot of places to see. It would

be fun to retrace some of my moves with you along, and as a civilian.

Must close now. If you don't hear from me for some time, don't worry and write often.

Love,
Bill

P.S. Sent a trunk-locker with a lot of my things in it to Jean. Take anything you want. I won't be needing it anymore.

B.

On March 16, Bill and the rest of the 142nd regiment moved to Camp Dix, New Jersey. From there it would join the rest of the Division at the New York Port of Embarkation.

March 27, 1943

Dear Mom,

Just a line to tell you my new address. Tell every one in Montana hello for me. Wish that I could be going back with you.

Had a letter from Frank. He and Mary have separated. He didn't say what the trouble was, just that they didn't get along. He's living at the Detroiter Hotel now, but is going to move to an apartment as soon as he can find one.

I'll let the allotment ride the way it is. Hope the bonds start arriving. As far as I know, all of my affairs are in order, which is a commendable state of affairs. Uncle Don writes once in a while. Doesn't say much. Had a letter from Dad. He seems to be all-right. He says even less than Don, but he doesn't use as much stationary to do it.

Be sure that you write down my address and don't lose it, it may be quite awhile before I can give it to you again.

That's all for now. Will try to write more later.

Love,
Bill

March 29, 1943

Dear Jeanne,

By all means, use anything in the locker that you wish. That is why I sent it to you. Hope the things can do you some good. Please save the folder that is marked 201 File. I may need it if I ever get back to the States.

"Omnis Gallid est in tres partis divisa." My beloved "Caesar" is swell reading, if you're interested in tactics, which you aren't. The only book I'm taking with me is a copy of Shakespeare.

Guess Donnie didn't get the knife mailed. At least I failed to receive it.

My correspondence with Bettie has sprung up again, with one change however. My letters are as matter-of-fact as hers. Could be the heart break is all over. She and Jean Boyle are burning a candle for me at St. Aloysius Church as soon as they can find a Catholic friend to tell them the procedure. Bettie is donating blood to the Red Cross and says that she hopes that some of it will be reserved for me, just in case. I don't think our blood types are the same however. For your file I am "A" type.

Say hello and good bye to everyone for me. If you can get in touch with Vick I'd like to have him write to me. Do you ever hear anything about Roy Levering?

Best of luck to you and the boys—all three of them.

Love,
Bill

On Friday, April 2, 1943, the 36th Division, traveling in five transport ships, departed New York Harbor for Oran, Algeria. The 142nd left from pier 13 on the *Argentina*.

There was entertainment on the trip over. The ship's paper, the *Twin-Ocean Gazette*, ran a story on an "all-soldier variety show" that featured "slap-stick comedy, jive, red-hot rhythm, and semi-classics . . . . " Part of the entertainment was

two solos by 2nd Lt. Robert Cromwell, who formerly sang for N.B.C. and C.B.S. and appeared in

Broadway musicals which included 'Brother Rat' and 'New Wine.' The Lieutenant studied music at the University of Arizona and in New York.

The men also enjoyed the 142nd regimental band directed by Warrant Officer Irving Young, "former Decca recording arranger," and entertainment by Pfc. Jack Miller, a "personality" drummer who "formerly played behind the famous singer Hildegard."

The Division arrived in Oran, Algeria on Tuesday, April the 13th.

VI
I'm Actually in North Africa

[V-Mail]

April 22, 1943

Dear Mom,

The last letter you had from me was written in the
states, but this one really comes from the other side. I'm
actually in North Africa. It's almost too good to be true.
We've moved once since we arrived, but not far. I like it
over here very much. The country itself is beautiful. A lot
like where you are now. The natives are a mixture. Some
French, some Berber, some Arab, and polyglot of other
nationalities. The French are very nice. I'm trying to learn
to speak the language and not doing badly either. The
Arabs and Berbers are miserably poor and filthy beyond
description. The little kids run alongside us on the road
and beg for "un cigarette, American." Some of the little
girls, not more than ten years old, carry their baby
brothers and sisters (I presume) slung to their back in a
sort of shawl. Saw Father Quinn and my old Colonel
again. Went into one of the towns a week ago and ran
into Gerhard Rehder. He was in my class at Benning you
know. We had a grand reunion and drank quarts of vin
blanc. White wine to you, Butch. I expect to see my old
friend, Ray Allen. He's over here some where, and "all
roads seem to lead to Rome." Not far from us there are
several old forts. The old strong-holds of the French
Foreign Legion. Those soldiers certainly were acquainted
with the Napoleonic maxim, "if you would control the
valleys, control the heights." The forts sit on hill-tops and
the cleared valley sweeps away from them for miles in
every direction. There is nothing left of them except the

walls and a few buildings, but from a distance they have
every appearance of life, and you expect to see a troop of
horse men come wheeling out as you approach. I've
found a lot of men to play chess with, and most of them
have sets of their own, so I won't miss my set much. I've
improved to the point where I can give the Regimental
Chaplain a run for his money. Bob Cromwell and I
attended the Jewish Passover services, which pleased Dr.
Rosenberg muchly. They insisted that we accept some
matzos, an unleavened bread that is almost tasteless. We
accepted and proceeded to eat it while we drank a bottle
of sacramental wine that one of the Catholic Chaplains
had given us. I received the cigarettes from Mae and I
think that I had time to write to her saying thank-you.
Are you receiving the bonds yet? It's been almost nine
months since I paid for the first one. We received all our
pay over here in Franc notes. An American bill-fold was
never designed for this size money. We go around
bulging. I've had my first ride in the old French 40 ot 8
box-cars. They are ridiculously small. Anything like them
in the States would be laughed off the tracks.
Incidentally, the French words for railroad are, "chemin
de fer." I always thought that was a gambling game. I'm
in good health and reasonably happy. Certainly I'm busy.
Don't worry about me, I can get along anywhere. You
would have enjoyed seeing me converse with the French
with the aid of a French-English dictionary and a lot of
excited gestures. That's all for now.

Love,
Bill

Gus Rehder, Bill's OCS classmate, recalls meeting Bill and
Bob Cromwell in Oran on April 17, 1943. Two days later Gus
made an entry in the journal he kept in North Africa:

I finally met a lot of my Benning classmates here,
and the other night met, by arrangement, my one
particular friend—a chap from Montana, a very clever,

cynical and amusing person—the one really 'civilized' member of the class. We had a great reunion. Unfortunately he has already moved on, but we shall doubtless meet again. We picked Budapest when we drank our toast to the next reunion.

Gerhard Rehder

On April 18, 1943, Bill's outfit moved from Oran, via the "ridiculously small" French railroad, to Magental, Algeria, approximately eighty miles away. General Walker wasn't as generous as Bill in his description of the railroad. The General called it "dinky... slow, unreliable, and crowded." In May the 142nd moved to Tlemcen, in the mountains of Algeria.

Bill's chess game with the Regimental Chaplain, Herbert E. MacCombie, was not insignificant. Chaplain MacCombie and Corporal Swartz were recognized as the two best chess players in the Division. They represented the 36th Division in a tournament held on July 25, 1943 between the 36th Division and a group of prominent Arabs near Rabat, Morocco—and beat all opponents!

"V-Mail" had been introduced by the War and Navy Departments in June of 1942 as a supplement to regular mail service. It was designed to save the weight and bulk of normal mail. A letter, either to or from a serviceman, was written on special forms. There was an address block on the top and a place for the censor's stamp. The text of the letter was written in the space below, but limited to one side of the sheet. The finished letter was turned in for processing. It was photo-

graphed on microfilm and flown overseas. Once the letter
arrived, it was reproduced on special "V-Mail" paper, five by
four inches, folded and put into special window envelops and
delivered as regular mail. Reproduction on such small paper
made small handwriting difficult to read. Additional sheets
had to be done on the same forms. "V-Mail" was faster than
regular mail (a little slower than "Air Mail") but often limited
how much was written and lacked the personal touch of a
"real" letter. Naturally, the "V" was for Victory.

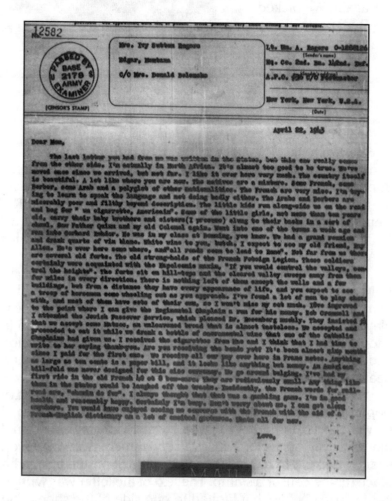

V-Mail, actual size

May 20, 1943

Dear Mom,

This would probably take longer to reach you than it would if I used V-Mail, but I wanted to write a long letter while I have time. None of your letters that I have received so far have my overseas address on them so you can judge about how fast the mail is traveling.

I've seen several of the towns in North Africa and now that I have acquired enough French to make myself understood, I like it quite well. Wouldn't trade any of them for Billings on Saturday night tho. At eight-thirty sharp everything closes up tight and the stores all roll down heavy metal shutters so that even the downtown districts look like a row of garages.

A few days ago I went into a town with the Regimental band and went to the dance for which they were playing. I soon attached myself to an Army Nurse named Bernice Ross. Just being with a woman that spoke American was such a rare treat that for a little while I forgot that I was in a foreign country. I got another nurse named Robby Scott, for Mr. Young, the Warrant Officer in charge of the band. At eleven-thirty we had to leave them, so Mr. Young went out to where the band was sleeping and I went to the Foreign Legion Officer's Club and had a few drinks and a lot of conversation until about four in the morning. Then they fixed me up with a grand room in the Officer's Quarters. The next day we got the nurses and rode around to see a real Mohammedan Mosque, then we had him drive us to the city park and we wandered around there until it was time for us to leave. We had a grand time, better than it really was I suppose, because of the comparison with the life that we had been living.

If I can I am going to send you some souvenirs of this country. They make some very beautiful costume jewelry from beaten silver, the kind you like. I want to get a tapestry and a native rug too. I'd like to send you some of the local money but the censorship rules forbid it.

There are a few spots in this country that are even more gorgeous than anything that I have seen at home.

Probably because they are not cluttered up with
hamburger stands and billboards.

I have a couple of rolls of film that I am going to send
to the photographer censor. He'll mail you the developed
film but no pictures. You can have whatever prints you
want made and I'd like you to send me a strip print of
them. You know the kind I mean. They are the same size
and shape as the negative and are in a roll. Will you send
all the 35 millimeter film that you can get? It's apt to be
scarce so try everywhere, even Sears Roebuck.

Just received a letter from Uncle Don full of the usual
trivia. I wish he could write a letter that didn't read as
tho he had to let someone he personally disliked censor it.

Jean writes once in awhile, but still no word from
Donnie. Tell him that if he doesn't write that I'll kick his
britches when I get home. Hope he goes to school as he
planned. He needs the education more than I ever did.
Incidentally Don writes that Doris Miller has married a
Tech. Sergeant on the west coast named Dahl.

I'm having them check on the bonds from this end
again. Seven fifty dollar bonds is not chicken feed to me
and I don't intend to lose it. Just found out that you will
not receive my new allotment (total $125) until the first of
June. I guess it will be there by the time you get this.

Had to let this letter wait for a day while I went on
what the Army calls a mission. Received another letter
from you in the meantime. Dated April 30.

The more I see of this country, the more I am amazed
by its beauty. The mountains, while not high are steep
and rugged. The valleys are patch works of green and
brown and occasionally a field that has been taken over
by wild poppies, show a vivid red against the pattern.

So glad that you like being back in Montana. Wish
that I could be there with you. I don't think that it will be
as long as I used to think. The African Campaign ended a
couple of weeks before I thought it would. Things seem to
be breaking our way at last. Our ability to mass produce
is finally piling up a tremendous edge in war implements.

Incidentally, if you can, send along some colored film.
I think that koda-chrome is the trade name, but any

colored film will do. This scenery certainly needs
photographing.

Every once in a while we tune in on the short wave
and listen to a propaganda broadcast from Germany. It's
called "your girl friend from Berlin." Maybe you can catch
it. It's beamed for North Africa, but you might be able to
pick it up. It will come on about one or two o'clock in the
afternoon in Montana. The Germans certainly don't
understand American psychology. She plays American
dance records with lots of Bing Crosby, with the intention
of making us home-sick, whereas it only makes us more
content to be here, since it serves as a reminder of all the
things that we are fighting for. At intervals she asks us
what we are fighting for and reminds us in very honeyed
words of the swell times we could be having with our
girls back home. Then of course we are constantly
reminded that the Jews are behind all of this for their
own selfish purposes, and all the time she is talking I am
standing with my arm looped over the shoulder of Mr.
Young, a Jew and one of the grandest men I have ever
met.

Tell every one hello and especially to Roy and Hazel
MacKenzie. Tell them I think of them often and would like
to write but am so limited in time and stationary that I
doubt I will be able to do it.

Guess that's all for now Mom. It's getting late and I
have to make a long trip tomorrow. I'm trying to build a
new sight for the 37 mm gun. The Regimental C.O. is
interested in it and has given me permission to build a
model so that it can be tested. I have several more ideas
and if this one works I am going to ask permission to try
them.

Good night Mom. Write as often as you can. I love to
hear from you.

Love,
Bill

June 7, 1943

Dear Mom,

I have had three letters from you. One regular dated the 12th, and two V-Mail dated the 17th and 24th. They all arrived within a couple of days of each other.

The stationary is grand and I wish you would send it to me. I can get packages now. And please hurry the 35 mm film. This country is crying to be photographed. Get some color film too if you possibly can. You may be able to get it by ordering it from California by mail.

I had a date yesterday, with a nurse. We rode around for a couple of hours in a carriage, had a couple of drinks and then had dinner. Afterwards we sat in the shade in a very pleasant garden and just loafed for a couple of hours. Life isn't so bad here but I'll trade all of it for six hours in Billings.

It seems impossible that it can be cold in Montana, its so blazing hot here. I don't mind it tho. Every time I begin to feel critical about the heat I think of last winter in Massachusetts and I shut up. I froze my ears several times and my nose and chin and once I even froze my upper legs. So it will have to get much hotter than this before I complain.

I have a couple of address that I want to keep and I may lose them, so I'm going to write them here and I want you to save them for me.

Chuckry Bey
c/o Caid de Gabes, Tunisie

Sergeant Meghelli
36 C ie, 6 T.T.A.
Tlemcen, Algeria

Civilian - Allee de Sourus
El-Kalaa - Tleman, Algeria

Thanks a lot.

Yes, we know all about the war over here. No radio or newspaper but we get around.

Glad that the ranch is finally bringing you in some money. It's about time that it started paying off. Incidentally, now that I am sending $125 a month, I want you to put most of it in the bank. Buy one $50 bond a month, but bank the rest. When I get home I'm going to need some cash fast.

I'm glad you are going to have the little house. I want some place to come home to after this little affair is over.

Have a letter from Dad and one from Jean Boyle. Both written about the middle of May. Dad knows where Chris is and what outfit he is in. If he's in North Africa and I had his address I might be able to look him up. I get around quite a bit.

Oh yes, I'm a member of the "short snorter" club now. You have probably read about it.

Finally located a local woman to do my laundry, a stone lined irrigation ditch to bathe in and borrowed a litter to sleep on, so I'm living in the laps of the Gods. A soldier can ask no more. A clean body, clean clothes and a place to sleep that does not include rocks.

Tell everyone hello for me. Wish I could be there to see them all again, but that will have to wait a little while. When I come home I will amaze you with the fluency with which I speak French.

> J'ai vous adore!
> Bill

The "Short Snorter" Club? The September 6, 1943 issue of *LIFE* shows servicemen with yards of paper currency from different countries, strung together. The bills are called "short snorter bills," and the men are in the "club." They try to get everyone they meet, who belongs to the "club," to sign their string of bills and, of course, they sign the other club member's "short snorter bills" too.

While newspapers from the States were only available by mail, the *Stars and Stripes*, a soldier weekly originally published during World War I, had resumed publication in London on April 18, 1942. Designed to furnish officers and men with news about themselves, the first production was distributed throughout the British Isles each Sunday. Publication in Algiers began on December 9, 1942. The "Algiers Daily" version began on April 15, 1943 and the "Oran Daily" on May 3, 1943.

US Fliers with short snorter bills.

Photo by Thomas McAvoy/ LIFE Magazine © TIME Inc.

[V–Mail]

June 9, 1943

Dear Jeanne,

Can't understand you're not getting any mail from me. I've written at least four since I've been over here, not a great many, but certainly not the stoic silence that you imply. I refer to your letter on May 4th, which just arrived.

Tried to read Joyce's "Web and the Rock." Didn't like it. Might like Finnegans' Wake if I could get it. Most of my reading is confined to Shakespeare. I carry him where-ever I go and that includes some rather fantastic places. Wish I could show you some of those places. I know you would be thrilled by this country and the people. Incidentally, I now speak rather fluent French. Isn't that amazing. It's easy to learn when you have to in order to converse at all.

Don't know whether or not I asked you before, but just in case I forgot, please send me some 35 millimeter film. Black and white or colored. I know it will be hard to find but make every effort. I shall hate to leave this country without having some of it recorded on film.

Wrote a song lyric that may eventually be set to music and even published.

Verse:

A cocktail or two, the memory of you,
and I get as blue as the sea.
The sound of your name is part of the game
that fortune is playing on me.

Chorus:

The way we used to dance together
and laugh about the rainy weather
are part of the pain,
that keeps aching in vain—where to from you?

The echo of your voice is haunting,
the memr'y of your kiss is taunting.
Where-ever I go,
I'll be lost till I know, where to from you?

You were the moon and the starlight,
the end of my search for a dream.
I should have known that the starlight
would fade and you wake from a dream.

The shadow of your arms enfolds me.
Your funny little laugh still holds me.
If I can't have you darling,
what shall I do? Where to from you?

How do you like it? A simple thing, but mine own. It
isn't as grand as the Marseillaise, or as catchy as Dinah,
but like Mercutio's wound, it will suffice.
Time presses, write soon.
> Love,
> Bill

"Mercutio's wound." From *Romeo and Juliet*, Act III,
Scene I. Bill did enjoy his Shakespeare.

June 25, 1943

Dear Mom,
Will you take some of my money and buy me a watch.
Pay about twenty-five or thirty dollars for it. I lost the
cheap watch I had and am unable to purchase another
one over here. Hope you have already sent me some 35
mm film. I am anxiously awaiting it. Jean promised to
send me some too, but it hasn't arrived yet.
We've moved since I last wrote you and will move
again in a few days. This is a horrible area, so I won't be
unhappy about it. It is very dry and dusty here and about
nine o'clock every morning the wind starts blowing and
doesn't let up all day. We are fairly easy to clean but our
clothes and our guns are a problem.
Sunset in this country is thrilling and the sky
afterwards is a deep cerulean blue and the stars look like
gems. Much as it is in Montana except for the
unbelievable depth and richness of the night sky. It is
always cool at night so that we sleep soundly. The actinic
rays of the sun are hardly filtered at all, so we are all
turning a deep mahogany color where the flesh is
exposed.
We're putting on a command performance today. You
may read about it later in LIFE magazine. It's the sort of
thing that they print. It won't take too long, but it is
nicely calculated so that we will be a couple of hours late

for supper. However, if that is the worst thing that ever happens to us, we can consider ourselves the favored of the Gods.

I sent Dorothy a pair of native slippers. They are not much, but they are what the better class Arabian women wear. I sent you some costume jewelry. It is made of silver and is quite black, so you will have to have it cleaned.

No, I haven't seen anyone that I know over here except Gerhard Rehder. Ray Allen is here somewhere, but I haven't located him as yet. At the rate we're moving around the country tho, he can't evade me much longer.

No complaint on the food. It isn't asparagus tips on toast by a long ways, but considering the difficulty of supply, we are eating very well. Any one at home that thinks he is being severely rationed should spend a few weeks over here. Even wood for fuel is on the list and every day the items available to the lucky holders of ration cards are posted on bulletin boards, around which, excitable crowds gather. Things should be a great deal easier after the crops are harvested this fall.

Are there any good looking girls in Montana any more? These few months overseas have gotten me into a marrying mood. Maybe I'll bring home a nice Fraulein from the Fatherland. It's a cinch I won't bring a French girl. What a crummy race they are.

Give Chris my address and tell him to write to me.

Love,
Bill

P.S. Tell Donnie to write.

Back in the United States there was some labor unrest. In May, union boss John L. Lewis' coal miners walked out. Since coal kept the war material production lines moving, it was critical to the war effort. The Secretary of War dispatched armed troops to guard against violence and sabotage and to insure that miners who wanted to work could do so. The Secretary of the Interior took possession of the mines to operate them on behalf of the government. However, the coal strikes continued for the next few months. Lewis was blasted for giving aid and comfort to the enemy. Bill and the rest of the troops overseas read all about it in *The Stars and Stripes*—and were not happy with the miners.

June 27, 1943
Somewhere in North A.

Dear Mom,

This is Sunday and I haven't a thing to do, so I'm going to try to write a long letter. We are going to leave here tomorrow and we have been given the day to get our clothes and equipment in shape and to rest up. I've finished with my straightening up and am ready to leave on five minutes notice, so I don't feel guilty about laying around.

The day before yesterday several of us went to town and had a turkish bath. It isn't very much like the ones we have in the States, but it was certainly refreshing. You are provided with a large wrap-around towel and then you enter the steam room. After you have heated up enough to sweat profusely, a little gnome of an Arab grabs you and forcibly sits you down on a mat and cracks all your joints. Then he scrubs the hide off you with a big, rough mitten and soap. When that is through, you take a cold shower and it's all over. It cost twenty-five francs or fifty cents. It's a vigorous workout but afterwards you feel as relaxed as a baby.

Had to interrupt this letter for a while, while I helped the Co. C.O. work out the plan for the move. This is one phase of the science of Logistics. Every thing must be worked out before hand in complete detail. It is one of the toughest jobs (and the most thankless) in the army. Not just with a company, but when dealing with Divisions and larger units. In order to keep traffic flowing without interruption it is necessary for the convoy to pass given points at specified times and to maintain certain speeds and intervals between vehicles. The amount of food necessary for the trip must be calculated exactly, provisions made for a supply of water. Stops must be planned to permit the men to relieve themselves. The order of the vehicles in the column must be determined. For instance the last vehicle should always be the maintenance truck so that it can service any truck that breaks down. The medical truck must be near the rear so that they will be handy in case of an accident. The lead truck must have the march unit commander in it so that he can regulate the speed between points. The large trucks should normally proceed the smaller ones because the small trucks tend to out run the big ones if they are in the lead. A million little things like that all have to be planned out in detail. You can imagine the confusion that must be straightened out when planning for a big movement. The job done by General Somerval, the chief of the S.O.S. (Service of Supply) in planning the logistics of the big invasion fleet that took Africa is probably the biggest single job ever tackled. That is the thing that held the invasion time back so long. The troops were ready, but the public couldn't understand what to them seemed an unnecessary delay. Now you know all.

A big argument is going on in this tent about the coal strikes. We're pretty well decided that shooting is the best solution. We put a quick stop to that strike at North American. They decided that they weren't nearly as anxious to strike as they had thought, after they felt the end of our bayonets. I think that there will be a little job of settlement after the troops come home.

Had a nice time in town yesterday. Played some chess and ping pong at the Officer's Red Cross, then had dinner at the Officer's Mess. Watched part of an outdoor boxing match and then went to an American movie. The title was Icecapades. Not very good, but compared to these French movies it was a real treat. After the movie we stopped at the Red Cross again and I met a fellow that had been in my class at Benning. He's in one of the parachute outfits. He hadn't seen anyone from the class until he ran into me.

My new sight for my guns is a success. We tried it out yesterday. Now all I have to do is demonstrate it for the Regimental C.O. and I think that he will have my platoon equipped with them. After we have tried it out in combat, I think that I will write an article about it for the Infantry Journal.

The trucks have arrived and I have gotten the men started loading. It gives me a little time because all I have to do is check on the work once in a while. Forgot to mention. There was an interruption in this letter while I had dinner and then I took a couple of my non-coms and went out to the range where we fired yesterday and looked over the impact area. We weren't able to do it yesterday because there was other firing going on. The results are very satisfactory. The targets were a mile and a half away and if they had been the German machine-gun emplacements that they represented, they would have been completely wiped out. Then I read King Richard III from my Shakespeare. When the loading is finished I am going down to the shower and take a bath. You certainly need one in this country. The ground is as dry as powder and the wind blows constantly. At our next place I'll be able to go swimming every day in salt water. I'll like that. I haven't done that since the time I was in Ventura, California after the Fifteenth had been on strike duty at North American Aircraft.

Had a letter from Jeanne yesterday. Not much of a letter. I don't like V-Mail very much. It's so short. Just about the time the letter begins to get interesting, it's all over. She wanted to know if I had seen any action. The answer is no. Not at the front. By the time we had arrived they had it about sewed up and didn't need us. We've had a little excitement but I don't think that I can go into any details until a much later date.

Would like to have a picture of you on a horse if you can have one taken. I don't know just what the circumstances are over there. They have the necessary chemicals here, but I have no paper at all. Films, of any kind, are unobtainable. I'm enclosing a few postcards. I had to remove the identifying names, but I'll tell you all about the places when I get home again. The women actually dress the way you see them in the pictures. Just one eye exposed. We call them "Veronicas." Once in a while they have an accident, trying to watch something in one direction while walking in another.

The sun hasn't been too hot today so I spent part of it in my bathing suit, getting a little tan on the covered parts of my body. My face and hands are so dark that I looked awfully silly when I had stripped. A few weeks of sun will fix that. It isn't as hot here as it is in Montana, but the sun burns you a lot quicker.

Lt. Curran, the one we called "killer," has been transferred to a line company and Lt. Atkins now has the Ammunition and Pioneer Platoon. Lt. Crow, who at one time was our Bn. S. 4 (supply officer), was transferred from H. Co. to take Atkins' place as Transportation and Executive Officer. I had hoped a little for the job myself, but am very well satisfied with Crow. He knows his job and is a darned good fellow to boot.

I had hoped to make this a longer letter, but they want to pack the typewriter so I'm going to have to quit. They just moved the desk out from under the typewriter and I'm holding it on my lap. I'm in the best of health, as you might know, and having a pretty good time all things considered. Write when you can.

Love, Bill

The 142nd moved to Arzew, Algeria for amphibious training—and saltwater swimming!

(V-Mail)

July 6, 1943

Dear Mom,

Your letter of the thirteenth arrived several days ago, but I had just written you a long letter and had nothing to say, so I neglected answering it till now. I've been fairly busy lately. The usual routine incident to establishing the outfit in a new location. We'll probably move again very shortly but we always work on the assumption that we are going to stay put for a while, and try to make ourselves as comfortable as possible.

I'm in the best of health and enjoying myself muchly. If I could go without my clothes long enough to get my body as brown as my hands and face are, I don't think you would recognize me. The African sun is hotter than blue blazes. We have been able to swim in the Mediterranean the past week or so. It's delightful. Wish we had time enough so that I could spend a whole

afternoon there. We call it the North African Riviera. The
part that we use is just a little thing, and it is necessary to
crawl down a hundred and fifty foot cliff to get to the
water, but we don't mind, much.

Received a lot of letters today. From Bettie, Jean B.,
Mrs. Buckley and the girl I used to run around with when
I was an enlisted man in Seattle, Genevive Taylor. I'd like
to answer all of them tonight, but I'm afraid that the light
won't last long enough. Buckleys' have a cottage on Lake
Washington and have invited me to spend a vacation
with them. I think that was very nice of them, but I also
think that it is getting a little too optimistic about the
whole thing. This war is going to take several years yet,
and I don't intend to come home till it's through. I want to
be in the army of occupation and after that I want to go to
the Pacific and get in on the scrap over there.

Life over here is pleasant enough, all things
considered, but I have learned something. It isn't the big
things that you miss when you were away from home.
You expect to do without the important things, the people
you love, the place you like to be and that sort of thing.
It's the little things like a cold coke-cola or a hot shower
that you miss. We do our duty automatically but in the
back of our minds we are always trying to figure out a
way to be a little more comfortable and a little cleaner.
When we are living in pup tents, as we are at present,
and see other troops living in pyramidal tents, we mutter
something about desk soldiers and male wacs, but just as
soon as we get into pyramidal we start trying to figure a
way to get a floor in it.

Must close now and answer some of this other mail.

Love,
Bill

On July 10, 1943, the Allies invaded Sicily. The 36th Division
had originally been scheduled to participate in the invasion.
However, British General Montgomery requested that, instead
of the 36th, a Division with battle experience be substituted
and the 1st Division got the job. Bill's old outfit, the 3rd Division

from Fort Lewis (and thus Bill's friend Ray Allen), also made the invasion as part of General Patton's Seventh Army.

July 20, 1943

Dear Mom,

I've neglected writing for several days because I was sick but I'm all right now so I'll try to catch up. Your last letter was dated the 7th of July.

Am so glad that you were able to send me some film, and kodachrome too. Send black and white too, if you can get it. Dad and Jean are trying to get me some. Sure hope they do. I think I'm going to be over here a long time and once the present supply of film runs out there won't be any more.

I can get along very well on the thirty dollars a month that I have left after the allotment is taken out. If you remember, I always need to spend just whatever I happen to have in my pocket, so I'll try to keep the money in my pocket to a minimum. I'll need all the money I can scrape together after the war to start my store. After I get it going, we'll get a car and take a trip all over the States and into Mexico if we have enough time. We'll have a lot of fun, just the two of us. I got around the States quite a bit before I came overseas, so there are a lot of places I want to show you.

Can't understand what Donnie is doing. Isn't he working at all? Tell him to write to me. It sounds as tho he needs a good kick in the trousers.

I'm about six hundred miles west of Jack Bird, so I don't think I'll get to see him. Ray Allen is on Sicily. Wish I were with him. Guess I'll get my chance later.

We can go swimming in the Mediterranean almost any time we want to, so I am having a grand time. We're working hard, of course, but that is to be expected.

Wish I could get my hands on a deep dish apple pie.

The finance dept. says that the bonds should start arriving. Let me know when you get them.

I sent two rolls of film to the photographic censor in Washington to be developed and forwarded to you. Did you ever get them? When you do, I want you to send me strip prints of them. I can't remember what they are now.

Could use a pair of moccasin type bedroom slippers, rubber leather soles, if you can get them. Size 5 1/2 or 6-C.

How much money have I got in the bank now? And how much in bonds? It should pile up pretty fast now. Why don't you use some of it to have electricity and running water and a bathroom put in the little house?

Guess this is all for now. Will write again soon.

Love,
Bill

The war had not been going well for Italy. Sicily was being quickly overrun. The mainland would be next and German assistance was uncertain. Many Italians were concerned that Germany was not so interested in defending Italy, as it was in defending Germany *from* Italy. The Italians were certainly disenchanted with Mussolini and the mess they were in. On July 25, 1943, Mussolini's own party voted him out. The next day the Italian King, to Mussolini's dismay, recognized the action as binding, forced his resignation, and then had him arrested.

July 26, 1943
Dear Mom,

The long letter you wrote on the 28th of June, containing the clippings of the Detroit riot, arrived yesterday. You had already repeated most of the news in letters which you wrote later, but which arrived as much as ten days ago. I haven't figured out just what it is that happens to the mail. Guess the gremlins have a hand in it.

Haven't received the film yet, but expect it any day. Packages always take a long time. Hope it arrives before long. I'm not going to be lucky enough to stay where I am for long.

Tell Mr. Mac that I'm sorry, but Persian rugs are unobtainable where I am. The local product looks like a cheap Navajo and usually contains a high percentage of cotton. If I ever get to the Middle East, I may be able to pick one up.

A month or so ago I sent two rolls of film to the Photographic Censor in Washington. They were supposed to develop the film, censor it and send it on to you. Let me know if you have it or not, and if you have, have some strip prints made and send them to me.

Your plans for the little house sound swell. Better fix me a room. I'm going to need some place to live when I get back.

About the money, when I get home I want to start that camera store right away and I'll need every cent I can get to swing it. At that I'll have to get some of the big wholesalers to run me on credit for awhile. Will need the cash mostly for rent, fixtures, advertising and to live on till the darn thing starts making a profit. I know I can make a success of it, but if I can get an exclusive dealership from "Argus" in Ann Arbor, I can practically corner all the school trade. Have a lot of promotional ideas and advertising schemes. The whole thing hinges on whether or not I can save enough money to hold on till it starts paying.

Tell Dor and Don hello for me and ask them why they never write. I've been overseas three months and nary a letter have I had from them.

I answer all of Dad's letters as soon as I receive them, but he doesn't write often and then it's just a few lines on a sheet of V-Mail. He's apparently all right and feeling well. He's a little tired of his job and would like to go overseas on some sort of construction job.

Bettie L. and Jeanne Boyle seem to be my most profuse correspondents. Don't know why they picked on me, but I get three or four letters from them every week. We write zany letters that wouldn't mean anything to anyone but us. We have a lot of private jokes that we rehash.

Finally had a short V-Mail from Jeanne Lyman, the girl I knew in Boston. She promised a long letter shortly. No letter from Mrs. Buckley for some time. She used to write pretty regularly.

My address is A.P.O. #36. We just used the other one while we were staging and coming across. I guess it's to confuse the enemy. We had more code no's than a movie star has proposals.

Just sent a bundle of clothes off to the laundry. I think this is the last one I'll be able to send for some time.

U.S. law won't let me send any plants or seeds into the states so I'll just have to tell you about the ones I see. There is one lonesome flower blooming in the sand by my tent. It grew from the sand to a height of eight inches in about five days. It has a thick, green reedy stalk and no leaves at all. It has several buds and they bloom one at a time and last only two days. The blossom is white and has a solid center and then has six thin curled petals that stick out around the center like this

It's very pretty but has no odor.

The poppies are all gone now. They were beautiful, but awfully fragile. As soon as you picked them the petals fell off.

Wish I could bring home some of these Arabian horses. They would sell for $500. We don't have anything in the States that can compare with them.

Have you heard the story of the soldier in the Tunisian Campaign who pulled the lanyard that fired a big artillery gun. He'd step up to the gun and say "Mr. Hitler—count your soldiers" then he'd jerk the lanyard. When he heard the explosion as the shell hit he'd say "Mr. Hitler—count your soldiers now!"

The war news is good. Musso the muscle has resigned and Sicily can't hold out more than a couple of weeks. Maybe we'll have this thing wound up by Christmas of '44. Sure hope so. Then a couple more years to clean up the Japs and we can go home again. One of our big topics of conversation is whether or not we can get a short leave in the States after we finish up in Europe and before we go to the Pacific. Everyone hopes so, but none of us really believe it. I've only been over three months and already life in the States is beginning to seem like a pleasant dream.

We'll need a car when I get home. I'd like to have a convertible coupe. But a regular coupe would do. You might keep your eyes open and if you find a bargain, pick it up. Nothing older than a '39 or '40 and be sure that someone looks it over to see if it is in good shape.

Can't think of anything more to write. I'm well and feeling fine. Not putting on any weight—but not losing any.

Write soon.

> All my love,
> Bill

The riot in Detroit had been violent. During the evening of Sunday, June 20, 1943, police were called to Detroit's Belle Isle Bridge to quell a "racial disturbance." The police were unable to handle the problem. Federal troops were called in the next night but the "disturbance" went on for three more days. Thirty-four people were killed, hundreds were injured. The German controlled Vichy-French radio, trying to capitalize on the situation, called the Detroit riots a "revolt" that was a reflection of the moral and social crises in the United States.

> July 31, 1943

Dear Mom,

Glad you sent the film and stationery. Hope they get here soon. Keep trying to get film. I can use all of it that you can get.

Haven't much to say but wanted to let you know I am all right. We're eating well, probably better than you are, and getting a reasonable amount of sleep. What we're doing isn't too difficult. I now have a canvas cot to sleep on, so I'm very comfortable. Every time we move I decide that I am carrying along a lot of unnecessary things, so once again I'm in the midst of trying to decide what to throw away.

Had a short note from Frank. He says that he has quit one of his jobs. Seems to be feeling all right. Are he and Mary going to divorce?

The way that money is piling up I'll have enough to start that store when I get home.

Say hello to Dor and her family for me.

You say that all the girls are gone. I can understand the fellows being gone, but where could the girls have gotten to. Don't tell me they all joined the Waac's. By the way, do you ever see or hear of Edna Weast? I'd like a letter from her.

I sent Bettie and Jean some presents at the same time I sent yours, and received a letter yesterday saying that they had received them so I presume that you now have yours. Hope you like it. May be able to get you a ring a little later. I'm a little inconveniently located right now, to make my purchases.

Have several letters to write and not too much time so I'll have to close for now. Write soon.

Love,
Bill

In Sicily, the Italians were surrendering and the Germans were retreating before Patton and Montgomery. The Germans' retreat included a stiff fight as part of their withdrawal plan. The British managed to enter Catania, Sicily on August 5, 1943, the same day the Russian army took the city of Orel back from the retreating Germans.

Meanwhile, the 36th Division was to get a combat mission at last, an amphibious landing on Italy. The operation was code named AVALANCHE. After considering the area north of Naples and the Port of Naples, Salerno Bay was selected as the best landing site. Generals Clark and Walker, along with Admiral Hall, made decisions regarding which beaches to use and the number of supporting troops necessary. Then there were mountains of "minor details" left to be worked out by their staff officers.

General Clark

...... (missing pages)

Later is right. It's now the night of Aug. 10. Received a
V-Mail from you, right after dinner, and then got so
busy that I couldn't finish this one. Hope you can get
the watch and don't forget the gloves.

No, I'm not in the unit you mentioned. My unit is
smaller by two.

Nice news about Mussolini. Wasn't it grand to hear
that Orel and Catania both fell the same day? There is
just a slight chance that the European war may fold
before spring. The Russians should smash clear to Poland
this winter.

I wired you for fifty dollars. By the time you get this I
should have it. Haven't been splurging. I lent one of the
Lt's some money and he hasn't paid it back yet and I
don't like the feeling of not having any money in my
pocket.

Mr. Young still hasn't written any music to my song
and I can't get to him to prod him about it. In the
meantime I have completed four verses of an Infantry
Hymn. I got tired of the Navy and the Marines, the Air
Corps and the Artillery all having songs, and the best
outfit of them all without one. Don't know whence comes
this urge to write. Did I have any literary ancestors?

Jean is a stinker. She only writes about every three
weeks. Haven't yet had a letter from Dorothy. Is her arm
broken?

You and Bettie L. and Jean Boyle are my most faithful
correspondents.

So glad that you are fixing up the little house. Why
don't you have all that ground on your side of the river
fenced in?

I spend some of my spare time figuring out the most
minute details of my projected business venture. Never
before, I think, has anything like it been given so much
prior planning. When I finally get home and get started, it
should run like clock-work and make me preposterously
rich in no time at all. Write soon.

Love,
Bill

(V–Mail)

August 12, 1943

Dear Mom,

Just wrote you a regular letter and then I received the V–Mail you wrote the 2nd of July. Sorry you went so long without receiving any mail from me. I guess you understand that there are times when I can't write. I always answer your letters as soon as I can after I receive them.

Yes, we eat a lot of dehydrated food. It isn't at all bad. The eggs aren't too good but they make nice French toast and things like that. I hope that eating dehydrated food is the worst thing I have to do in my life time. Packages to soldiers overseas only need postage to or from New York. The Army picks them up there and handles them without charge. Haven't spoken French in some time now and am beginning to forget how. The words and grammar are easy, its the damn accent that is difficult. If you don't pronounce the words exactly as they do, the stupid French refuse to understand. The war news continues to be favorable. Perhaps this thing will be over before long. Hitler ought to crack before long, or be removed by the high command, in an effort to secure a lenient peace. I imagine that Russia, Poland and Czechoslovakia will have something to say about that.

All my love,
Bill

The Regiment had left Arzew on August 11, 1943, boarded ships at Mers el Kebir, and undergone amphibious training on the 12th, 13th, and 14th. A night landing exercise was held on the 15th. They returned to Arzew on the 16th.

On August 17, 1943, Sicily fell to the Allies. After combined American and British forces broke through at Randazzo, four days earlier, the Allied drive resumed almost unchecked. The Americans and the British both made amphibious landings close to Messina. The 3rd Division (with Ray Allen) entered the city and were soon joined by the British 8th Army. The Germans had withdrawn according to their plan.

Planning for the 36th Division's part in operation AVA-LANCHE moved ahead at a furious rate. Correct combat loading of the Division and attached units, so as to insure unloading and delivery to the proper beach in the needed combat order, was critical. Frequent changes in loading schedules caused by inexperienced Army and Corps staff officers exasperated General Walker. Walker was very happy with the cooperation he received from Admiral John L. Hall, the operation's Naval Commander (for the Southern - American - Attack Force). He was also struck by the contrast between the Admiral's clean and pressed uniform, his clean orderly ship—with the beds, baths and meals—and the lot of the Infantry, living in the field, in tents. With all the recent amphibious training, Bill noted the contrast too.

August 19, 1943

Dear Mom,

Haven't a typewriter available so you will have to suffer my scrawl. Thanks a million for the stationary. It's grand—and such a lot of it too. I like having personal stationery. The picture is swell. It is much better enlarged than it was as a snap shot. Yesterday was a great day. I received your package, a package from Bettie and Jean, containing a saddle-leather picture folder with their pictures, four letters from them, one from Marylee and one from Donnie.

I'm as healthy as I can be, but I'm not very clean. The dirt around here blows constantly and it sticks to everything. Last night I took a bath in my helmet and put on clean clothes that had just come back from the laundry (a French family) and thirty minutes later, the inside of the collar was black or rather red. Spent a few days on a boat a while back. It was sure nice to eat at a table. It was almost too much when we discovered that we had white linen table cloths and a solid silver service. Remind me to join the Navy the next war!

Ray Allen got away before I got to see him. I presume you know where he is, his outfit has been in the news lately. May see him before the war is over. I'd sure like to count noses in that outfit. I had a lot of friends there.

The roll of color film arrived several days ago. Thanks a lot and thank Donnie for me. I'll save it till I can get some really good pics.

I stopped for a few minutes to read the new copy of LIFE. We get magazines pretty regularly over here. Of course they are a little old but that doesn't make much difference over here.

I expect the Axis to fold pretty fast for a while. We've got a lot of pressure on them and Hitler never knows where we are going to strike next. I thought that they would hold a final defensive at Messina, but when Randazzo fell the whole thing collapsed. The news from the Russian front is all good. I rather think that the Russ will put on a big offensive this winter. If they do, they will probably drive all the way to the old Polish border. As soon as Russia reaches the Baltic and Norway falls, Finland can get out of the war. Write when you can.

Love,
Bill

August 25, 1943

Dear Mom,

No letter from you in quite a while. Maybe I'll get them all in a bunch. That's the usual procedure. Haven't much to say. Just wanted to let you know that I was all right. Still healthy but rapidly losing my suntan.

Had a nice letter from Dorothy. She seems well and happy but I think she ought to have a little more fun. Home is a nice place but it can get awfully tiresome.

No letter from Dad for a long time. Hope he's all right. MaryLee wrote me. She's quite grown up now. Writes a very mature letter. Part of it was in French so I had to rack my brain to answer in kind.

No hope of my seeing Chris, at least at present. Wish I could. He's a swell fellow. Can't imagine him getting engaged tho. He never had much use for marriage. A little war will make a lot of changes in a man. I'm probably different, tho I can't notice it.

Whatever happened to Percy Hopper? Has he gone into the Army? It would be a miracle if they passed him up. Huck's getting married is no surprise. He'd marry the first girl that accepted him.

Have gotten rid of a great deal of the stuff that I was still carrying around and will probably get rid of a lot more before this thing is over. Every time we move I realize that I have a lot of unnecessary belongings. Surprising how little a man needs when he has to carry it on his back. Am keeping my dress uniform however. May need it for that victory parade in Berlin. I may lose them but if I need them after I return to the States, I can buy some more. Money doesn't have the value it used to, in the light of our present position.

About all I spend money for, any more, is in playing poker. If I continue to improve, it won't even take any money for that. I usually break even now. As soon as I learn that it is almost impossible to fill an inside straight I'll have it made.

I'm still in my old job and will probably remain in it for the duration. Incidentally, I'm pretty good at it. I am the accepted authority on my subject in my unit.

Nothing more to say. Write soon.

Love,
Bill

The purpose of Allied censorship of the mail was to prevent anything getting out which might furnish information of value to the enemy. Trying to preserve the element of surprise for the impending invasion of Italy was an impossible job. Still, they tried. As an overly zealous example that they meant the strict censorship rules, British Major General H.A. Freeman-Attwood, commander of the 46th Division, was replaced just two weeks before the invasion when a censor reported that the General had written a letter to his wife in which he said: "I hope I shall be drinking a bottle of champagne somewhere in Italy on our wedding day."

On August 26, operation COWPUNCHER started. Designed to simulate the upcoming Salerno landing, the regiment again boarded ships and at 0330 August 28, 1943 started landing on St. Lew beach. They continued inland toward their objectives until 1145 when the problem was called off.

August 28, 1943

Dear Mom,

Haven't heard from you for over ten days. Hope that nothing is wrong at home. I'm still healthy, but getting a little more lonesome for home every day. Roosevelt seems to think that this affair will be over by New Years. Can't see it myself, but I sure hope he's right.

Censorship is even more strict that it used to be, so my letters are going to be shorter and duller. You'll have to wait till I return to hear all the things I'm doing and the places I've been. Most of them were pleasant and the unpleasant ones don't appear so bad now that they are just memories.

Had letters from Jeanne, Frank and Mrs. Buckley today. None of them had much to say, but I was glad just to get a letter of any kind, so long as it came from the States. Guess the States aren't all pleasant and there are a lot of things that we don't like about the way things are run, but just the same, from this time and distance, America seems like heaven.

Dorothy said that Alvina had to have a Caesarean. Non compre. She was the last person I would have supposed that couldn't have her child normally. Hope she and the baby are all right now.

Frank said that they had a beautiful summer in Michigan. How was it in Montana? Hope they had a good crop. Lend-lease is feeding an amazing amount of people.

We'll see how good a prognosticator I am. I look for tremendous developments in Sweden, Norway, Finland and Turkey within the next few months. Maybe important enough to materially affect the war. This thing could break fast if the proper events occurred soon enough.

Heard from Dad. He's leaving Indiana. Didn't know where he would go from there. Seemed to think that he would like to go to China, but I doubt that he will. He just likes to think about doing that sort of thing.

Tell everyone hello for me. Must go now. I have work to do.

Love,
Bill

On August 31, 1943, General Eisenhower, accompanied by Generals Clark and Walker, reviewed the Regiment. And on September 3, the Regiment moved once again to Mers el Kebir to board the ships. Practice was over.

VII
Combat

On Sunday, September 5, 1943, as part of operation AVA-LANCHE, the 36th Division left North Africa and sailed for Italy. Lieutenant General Mark Wayne Clark, commander of the new American Fifth Army, directed the AVALANCHE operation. The Fifth Army was made up of the British X Corps and the American VI Corps. VI Corps consisted of the 36th and 45th Infantry Divisions. The 45th was to be held in reserve, and the "T-Patchers" were to make the initial American assault on the beaches.

This was to be the first landing by American troops on the continent of Europe. When he wrote the next letter Bill was aboard the USS *Joseph T. Dickman*, enroute to the landing at Salerno where he and the 36th were about to get their first combat experience.

Sept. 7, 1943

Dear Mom,

I don't have much time, so this probably won't be a long letter. Received two long letters from you the day before yesterday. That was the best mail-call I've ever had. Two letters from you, two from Bettie, one from Jean Boyle and one from Genevive Taylor, a girl I met when I was at Ft. Lewis, and I received in the same mail, two rolls of film from Bettie.

Your film hasn't arrived yet, but I expect it in a couple of weeks. I won't be able to use it before then anyway, as I haven't my camera with me right now. Glad you were able to locate a watch. I shall be looking forward to it. The film sounds swell. That should be enough to photograph everything in Europe.

I don't know the address of the department that
handles the bonds, but if you should decide to write
about them, write to the Finance Dept. U.S. Army, Wash,
D.C. and they will either take care of it or give you the
address.

Glad things are going so well at home. Take care of
yourself and have just as much fun as you can. Of course
I'll want you in Billings when I start out. I like to think
that I'm independent and capable but I find it lots easier
when somebody is encouraging me. Remember how I
used to bring my math problems to you when I was in
High School. That's what I need. Somebody to keep me
thinking straight.

I could marry that girl in Washington if I wanted to
but the way I feel now I don't think I'll get married for
quite a while. It's going to take me a long time to get
used to being a civilian again.

From the progress the Allies are making in Europe,
maybe it won't be too long until I can get into the Pacific
where I'd like to be.

Wrote to Chris, but no answer yet. The money sure
piles up fast. By the time you get this you should have
almost $500, not counting the bonds. I think that's pretty
good. Specially for me. I never could save a dime.

Don't worry about me Mom. I'm in good health and
can do a pretty good job of taking care of myself.

All my love,
Bill

On September 8, the literal eve of the attack, the Italians
surrendered. The Germans had anticipated an Italian surrender, however, and were well prepared to meet the Allied
invasion.

The 36th Division's attack plan called for the 2nd Battalion
of the 142nd Regiment to make their assault onto "Green"
beach at 0330, September 9, 1943. At 0310 Lt. (jg) Grady R.
Galloway, United States Coast Guard, commanding the guide
boat, located Green beach by sighting the torre di Paestum—a
medieval stone watchtower on the shore. Lt. Galloway began

blinking a green light seaward, guiding 2nd Battalion assault boats to their designated landing area. The fighting was fierce.

Second Battalion's Commanding Officer, Lieutenant Colonel Samuel S. Graham, had given his men a simple order—he wanted them all on top of their objective, Mount Soprano, by nightfall. As they landed the initial assault waves were met by heavy machine gun and artillery fire, much of it from the ancient stone watchtower. When it got lighter the Germans strafed and bombed the beaches. There were also tank attacks. Still, by the end of the day the 2nd Battalion had reached its assigned objective and was on Mount Soprano.

Lieutenant Colonel Samuel S. Graham, CO 2nd Battalion, 142nd Infantry

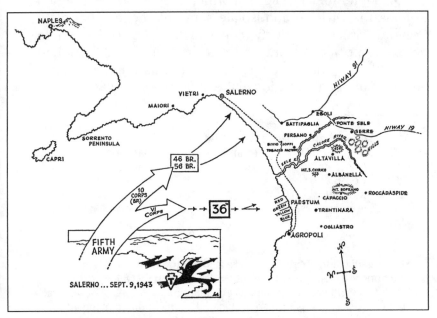

Allied invasion of Italy at Salerno, September 9, 1943.

The 142nd RCT (Regimental Combat Team) JOURNAL, a terse log[1] maintained by the Regiment during the fighting, has the following entries:

"10 Sept 1943 . . .

"1445   To 2nd Bn CO 'Request location of your Bn' . . .

"1545   Lt. Rogers, 2nd Bn. reported verbally location of 1st and 2nd AT Plats—at TEMPO DE SANPAULO . . . . "

On Saturday, September 11, German attacks against the British caused General Clark to shorten their line of responsibility and consequently lengthen the VI Corps responsibility. The 45th Division was inserted into the gap. VI Corps made an assault along the left flank of the American sector. During the afternoon elements of the 142nd occupied the town of Altavilla, almost unopposed. However, that night German patrols infiltrated their positions and on Sunday the 12th, Germans counterattacked in force.

On September 13, German armor and infantry threatened to flank the Division and isolate some elements. That night General Walker hurriedly consolidated the Division into defensive positions along La Cosa Creek. General Clark had the 504th Parachute Infantry dropped in as reinforcements. Second Battalion's position in the defensive line was one and

---

1   Abbreviations common to the JOURNAL are:

RCT	Regimental Combat Team	Bn	Battalion
Co	Company	AT	Anti-tank
Cp	Command post	Div	Division
Kil	Kilometer	Hqs	Headquarters
FO	Forward observer	Op	Observation post
Mg	Machine gun	Ldr	Leader
Arty	Artillery	Btry	Battery

Staff organization abbreviations are also common. Staff officers' functions are designated by numbers. 1 is Personnel Officer; 2, Intelligence Officer; 3, Operations and planning; 4, Supply. The general staff of division or higher is so designated by the addition of the letter prefix "G." G-2 would be division (or higher) Intelligence Officer. Regimental or battalion staff are designated by the letter "S." S-2 would be battalion or regimental Intelligence Officer.

one-half miles south of Albaella, protecting the right flank. Not everyone got the word to pull back that first night. In a May 30, 1990 letter, retired Major John R. Johnson, who on September 13, 1943 was an "E" Company platoon leader, remembered that:

> [a]t Salerno, when the Division was forced to withdraw into a tighter perimeter, the 2nd Bn. 142nd was ordered to withdraw at night from near Roccadaspide into the beachhead perimeter. "E" Company, 142, was overlooked and left behind. When daylight came and Captain Barnett became aware of the situation, he pulled the Company into rough terrain and sent out patrols to find 2nd Bn. After dark the following night, Lt. Rogers made contact with us and guided us back into the perimeter. We were up-tight and trigger happy by that time, and any attempt to contact us was a risky affair. Lt. Rogers had a loud voice when needed, that you could recognize as his own. From my location covering the rear of the Company, I heard him yell "E Company!" It was a welcome yell, and contact was made without incident. Had Lt. Rogers made an error in judgment, and had we not been "E" Company, we all would have been in a bad way. His voice that night was a most welcome sound.

The JOURNAL:
"15 Sept 1943...
> Lt Col Ainsworth talked with 2nd Bn. Cos E and H have joined the Bn... "

German armor attacked the La Cosa Creek line several times during the day on Tuesday the 14th. But the line held and destroyed numerous enemy tanks.

The JOURNAL:
"15 Sept 1943...
> 2nd Bn called that they have a motor patrol patrolling E and to ROCCADASPIDE...

Lt. Rogers reported at CP. patrol contacted
504th Parachute Bn had brought in 3 Italians
who reported about 3,000 Germans in groups
of from 10 to 50 men, also 3 Btrys. The men
were generally between POSTAGLIONE and
AUIETTA. The Btrys were about 1 kil out of
POSTAGLIONE. Also contacted a patrol of the
45 Div at point where road is blown. I made a
personal report to ROCCADASPIDE. I was in
the town and no Germans were seen along
the road. The local police said that there
were no Germans within 5 kilometers . . . . "

Roccadaspide, one of the objectives on the Salerno beachhead.

In his 1945 letter to Ivy, Corporal Charles W. Stimson
recalled the night when

[Lt. Roger's] patrol broke ahead of our front line
companies and entered the town of Rocca d'Aspide,
Italy, and were the first to move into the town. He
would often laugh about that and razz the rifle
company commanders.

Lt. Bob Cromwell was transferred toward the end of the Salerno operation. In a 1944 letter to Ivy he recounted his last meeting with Bill:

> [Bill was] coming down a dusty road in Italy—mounted on a jeep as if it were some massive charger—and with a submachine gun in his hand and a bandolier of ammunition around his waist. He was dirty and grimy and hot—but he yelled at me "how's the war going on?"—and I yelled back "you ought to know—you're doing most of the fighting" and he was gone—waving at me . . . .

Roccadaspide in 1991.

Former 2nd Battalion "H" Company Commander, Captain Terrell J. Davis, remembers an incident during the Salerno landing when Bill and his anti-tank "pop" gun saved the day for him. Captain Davis' men had been assigned to guard a crossroad. This brash young 2nd Lieutenant (Bill) arrived with a squad of men and their "pop" gun. They all saw five German tanks led by a motorcycle, moving up the road towards them. Bill said he would take care of them. Captain Davis says he had heard lots of young Lieutenants "talk" about what they were going to do, but this one made a believer out of him. Bill and his men went to work. With a BAR they killed the lead motorcycle driver and several of the tank captains who were up and looking out of their turrets. Effective use of the "pop" gun disabled or drove off the rest of the tanks. "H" Company had no weapons heavy enough to fight tanks

Captain Terrell Davis,
"H" Company

with. "Thank heavens he [Bill] was there and did such a good job." Obviously, this "accepted authority" was able to do the job in combat conditions too.

The Germans withdrew from the beachhead on September the 18th. That same day the 3rd Division came ashore. The 142 was relieved on September 21, 1943. Losses had been very high. They needed rest and replacements of both men and equipment.

General Clark was worried about a German parachute drop on his headquarters. On September 22, 1943, Bill's 2nd Battalion got the job of providing parachute defense for army headquarters at night. Since they were to be on the alert at night, General Walker relieved 2nd Battalion of its daytime training routine.

With actual fighting at least temporarily over, Bill's letter writing resumed. Censorship rules restricted the content.

[V-Mail]

Sept. 23, 1943

Dear Mom,

Nothing much happening that I could write about so haven't written for a couple of weeks. I'm well and contented, so don't worry about me. Wish I could be home for Thanksgiving, but guess that will have to wait. Roosevelt seems sure that this will be over by Christmas. Hope he knows what he is talking about. Haven't had any letters from you for some time, but expect they will all arrive in a bunch again. Lost my billfold. It only had thirty dollars in it but it had a lot of papers and pictures I miss. It was the big leather billfold that Dad gave me. Wrote to Chris but no answer. Ray Allen is near me now but haven't seen him yet. Talked to a couple of nurses a few hours ago. Hadn't seen any English speaking women for some time. It sure seemed good to talk English for a change. I have to struggle too hard when I speak some foreign lingo. Tell everyone hello for me. I'd sure like to see them again. All my love,

Bill

Sept. 28th

Dear Mom,

Received your V-Mail letter yesterday, written August 23. Haven't had any mail for several weeks, so it was doubly welcome. Received the two large packages of film and a small one. Thanks for sending them, even though I may not be able to use them. Some dirty dog stole my camera. Don't suppose I'll ever find out who it was. Sure wish I had it with me now. Lost my billfold too, about thirty dollars in it and of course my identification papers, pictures and a few souvenirs. My own fault, so I guess I can't complain. The drops on the paper are mosquito repellent, which doesn't seem to work against flies. I'm plagued with them. Wish I could be home now, the prospect of winter in the field fails to entice me. I'm a hot weather fan.

I'm in good health and outside of being bored to tears <u>right now</u>, I'm having a pretty good time. Thought you might like to know that your oldest son has his share of intestinal fortitude. Quod erat demonstrandum. (Translation for the censor, "that has been demonstrated.")

Am going to send a few personal souvenirs home in a little while. Keep them for me. Oh yes. What is the bank balance now? How much do I have in bonds and have any of those I bought through the Army arrived yet?

Lt. Cromwell has been transferred so I haven't anyone to torment right now. If you haven't already sent the money, forget it. I can make out all right. Can't understand W.U.'s failure to be able to send it tho. My cable had a return cable address on it. Doesn't matter anyway. Wish you could see the pipe I'm smoking now. It's eighteen inches long and has a bowl about the size of the end of my thumb. It was a gift. I seem to make friends where ever I go. Lucky, cause I have a lot more fun that way. Differences in language don't seem to be any barrier.

When I get home, we'll fix up the little house and the grounds. I want to plant some hedges and to build an old fashioned stone well, with a roof and bucket and rope and a windlass. And I want plenty of roses planted all over. Never see any over here and I sure miss them. We should be able to build a stable and keep a couple of saddle horses. Think I would like to face the house with stone and make it a little larger. I spend a lot of time thinking about the things I'd like to do. My sergeant says that no matter what time of the night he wakes up, he always sees me walking around smoking a cigarette or just sitting looking at the stars. Guess I'm getting a little lonesome for home. I've been gone quite awhile now. Started to sing "when the lights go on again, all over the world." What an optimist I am. Nice to think about anyway. Am wondering what Roosevelt and Churchill will pull out of their shirt sleeves next. They have held all the cards so far and seem to be playing them high wide and handsome.

A letter from Jean yesterday full of the usual. Haven't heard from anyone else for a long time. I suppose I'll get my mail all in a bunch. That's the usual procedure.

Will have a lot to tell you when I come home. But I've exhausted all non-censorable topics in this letter, so I'll close.

All my love,
Bill

Sept. 30, 1943

Dear Jeanne,

Your letter of August 24, arrived yesterday. Was glad to get it. I hadn't had any mail for some time. You said you were worried about not getting a letter from me for three weeks. There will probably be times much longer than that when you don't hear from me. Don't think anything of it. I'm all right and can take care of myself.

DeNoto's "Year of Decision" is an historical novel of the year 1846. He believes that this year, more than any other, shaped the destiny of America. It is a well written story and integrates a lot of here-to-for isolated historical facts. It deals principally with the Mormon immigration and the Mexican incident. The story of Donner Pass is particularly well handled. Don't miss reading it. It's grand entertainment as well as a good education in American history.

Not much I can write about so you will have to be content with these meager letters until such time as the censorship regulations relax a little.

About Xmas presents. If you could knit a couple of pair of heavy wool sock, size 10, that would be as nice a gift as I could think of. I'm afraid to carry anything valuable since my camera was stolen. Lost my billfold under some rather exciting circumstances. Will tell you about it after the war.

Love,
Bill

During the evening of September 30, 1943, British troops entered the outskirts of Naples and on October 1, the 82nd Airborne and the Rangers moved into the city.

Oct. 5, 1943

Dear Mom,
       Just received your long letter of Sept. 7, and the
V-Mail dated the 15th and am going to try to write you a
long letter. You'll have to excuse the writing as I'm laying
on my back in bed and using a flashlight for illumination.
About sending me packages! Up until a short time ago I
was able to get almost everything I needed, but this is no
longer true so I would appreciate a package now and
then, if you care to send one. Candy is highly acceptable
if it's not the hard kind. We get a certain amount of that.
What I'd really like is some home-made fudge if you can
get the sugar and don't worry about it getting stale. Over
here there isn't such a thing as stale candy. You just have
to soak some of it in your mouth a little longer than the
rest. I could use a carton of cigarettes once in a while.
Camels if you can get them. I would appreciate a bottle of
scotch, if it is obtainable. Practically anything but rye is
acceptable. I can't stomach that. Toothpaste, shaving
cream and things like that I can get plenty of. Would like
to have some more pictures of the family. I lost my billfold
awhile back and of course I had all my pictures in it. Oh
yes, I'd like to get some packages of food. Things the
Army doesn't feed, like fruit cake, small tins of fruit, ditto
some nippy cheese, small jars of preserves, even the
small cans of canned milk would be welcome. I think you
get the idea of the sort of things I mean. In the way of
presents it's more difficult. I could probably use a pair of
lined gloves or mittens this coming winter, and maybe a
couple of pair of heavy knitted wool socks (size 9 1/2). My
outer garments have to be G.I. so there is nothing doing
there. Could use a few suits of underwear. I don't like the
kind the Army issues and my civilian ones are wearing
out. I like the jockey type shorts and shirts put out by
Coopers under the trade name "Cooforms." Shorts size 28
M 30 and shirts size 34. You might go into my foot-locker
and send me my money belt. Have urgent need of some
colored pencils. The wax type for writing on celluloid.
Thought when I started writing that I would only name a
couple of things, but the longer I write the more I think

of. You must think I'm pretty greedy to fill several pages with things I would like to have you send me, but I don't want all these things at once by any means. Make the packages small and spread them out over a long period of time. Guess I'll just save space by listing some of the things that I could use and you can save this letter and when you feel the urge to send me a package you can refer to it for suggestions: O.K.?

A good map or maps of Europe.
Pocket books, particularly mystery or detective novels.
Boy Scout type pocket knife. The kind with a can opener, screw-driver, etc.
Cigarette lighter (no fluid, get one that will burn white gasoline) maybe one of those chemical ones if they will let you send the fluid thru the mail.
A decent fountain pen (I'm using a fifty cent model to write this letter).
A small sharpening stone.
A package of Brillo, if such a thing is available.

Guess that's all unless you can get a cheap ($10 - $15) camera that will take 35 MM film. Mine was stolen. Remember that a little package every three or four weeks is better than a great big one.

I sent Dad a pair of native slippers and just got a card from the post office saying that he had moved and left no forwarding address. Am going to try to have them sent on to you.

Tell that knothead Donnie to finish his schooling. He hasn't done anything I told him. If he can't get in the Army he might just as well be making some of those big wages in an airplane factory as fooling around. Will finish this tomorrow need some sleep now. G'nite!

Have a few minutes before my duties begin so will add a little to this letter. Don't worry about me or the American soldiers as a whole. We know now that we can whip Jerry where ever we find him even on ground of his own choosing. We're better than he is in every way including plain, old fashioned guts. I'll tell you some stories when I get home. Incidentally, don't ever let anyone tell you that the Coast Guard is a branch of service for slackers. Those boys have my unlimited admiration. They're doing a darned tough job and doing it well.

Pay no attention to the German propaganda it isn't even based on a partial truth any longer. We hear them once in awhile and have a good laugh over the transparency of their statements.

Have a new job now. Will tell you more about it at some later date.

It's getting a little chilly here nights and I guess the rainy season is about to start. Won't like that. Living in the field is comfortable in the dry summer but not at any other time. Must go now, more later.

Here I am again. Too bad about Lester Orr. Was he the old man at Laurel? Most of the Orr's are pretty well mixed up in my mind.

All the film has arrived but no gloves, watch or slippers as yet. Expect they will arrive shortly. Bettie and Jean are sending me another "surprise" but broke down far enough to tell me that it was something to wear. Bettie sent some more pictures of herself. She must feel pretty comfortable about me as one of the pictures made her look as though she had just swallowed a persimmon.

Wish you would let me know about once a month the status of my bank acct, and the actual value of the bonds I have. Never can remember and I can't keep your letters to refer to as I have no room. First time I ever saved money and I want to gloat over it and tell me what a good boy I am.

A letter from Frank. He has moved to an apt. and seems to be doing all right for himself. He mentions seeing Nada. I had almost forgotten her.

Can't help thinking that this thing will be over by next summer, but we'll probably have to stay another year or so as occupational troops. Won't like that unless I get to travel around a lot. Would enjoy seeing Europe. I find that I acquire a speaking knowledge of a language easily. Don't understand, I detested them in school. Interest factor I guess. Will write again soon. Take care of yourself and don't worry about me. Just hope I'm getting up among 'em! I like it!

> All my love,
> Bill

Bill's remarks about the Coast Guard were well taken. The Coast Guard had been transferred to the Navy Department on November 1, 1941. Many Coast Guardsmen ran the landing boats that put the infantry ashore at Salerno.

Lester Orr worked for the railroad in Laurel and had both his legs cut off in a train accident.

> Oct. 10, 1943

Dear Jeanne,

Thanks for the V-Mail of Sept 24. Not much I can write present time. Wanted to let you know that I am all right. Mother sent me, at my request, a wrist watch, slippers and a pair of leather gloves. They haven't arrived as yet and I am beginning to think that they were sunk on the way across. Hope not. There is still a chance that they will arrive. Mail delivery here is very slow and they may be held up somewhere.

Bettie and Jean Boyle continue to write regularly. Bett even sent some snap-shots. How about you doing the same. All of my family pictures were lost a short while back.

Must close now. Hope you are all well and happy. I think that we will have this thing finished before any married men and/or fathers have to go overseas.

> Love,
> Bill

[V-Mail]

> Oct. 15, 1943

Dear Mom,

Just a short line to let you know that I am all right. Don't need the money I asked for, so if it comes I will endorse it back to you and I want you to use it to buy

Christmas presents for me. I'll tell you what and for whom in a regular letter, later. I'm ahead financially because I broke a crap game last night. Made eighty dollars. Wish I could tell you more about our life but for the present, of course, I can't. Don't worry about me! I know that if you could see me you would know that I am O.K. The gloves, slippers and watch haven't arrived yet but I am looking for them any day now. Packages always take longer than letters. Donnie hasn't written for ages. Jeanne writes once in a while, but outside of you, Bettie and Jean Boyle remain my most faithful correspondents. Do you have Dad's present address. I'd like to write to him, but letters addressed to DuPont are sent back unclaimed. I sent you a long letter a few days ago and listed everything I could think of that would make suitable packages for me. If you don't get it let me know and I'll write it again. I need a shave and duty is rearing its ugly head so I'll close. All my love.

Bill

VIII
I Have a New Job

October 20, 1943

Dear Mom,

Yesterday I received your long letter of Aug. 31. Have had letters from you with a later date than that but they were just short V-Mail. The picture was swell. You look swell, and not nearly old enough to be the mother of an old man like me. I'll tell them all that I'm your younger brother when I get home. Don certainly looks well. He dresses pretty nicely now. Seems as though it were only a few weeks ago that you had to make him dress at all.

Have some news for you. I have a new job. I'm the Battalion Intelligence Officer now and was promoted to the rank of First Lt. on the twelfth of this month. Can't tell you any details now. Maybe I can later. I want you to continue addressing my letters to Lt. Rogers. A 2nd and a 1st are both called Lt.

Glad that Dad stopped to see all of you. Wish that I could have been there. It seems ages since I last saw the family and I suppose it will be a long time before we are all together again.

Don't worry about any expression of emotion in the family. We're just not the type. Don't care for it myself, but that doesn't affect my feelings. Too much gushing only impresses other people and I don't care what other people think about anything.

Don't understand the set-up on the film that I sent to the base censor. They were supposed to send the developed film to you. If you don't get it, you had better write to them. Looks as though someone had stepped out of line to me, but I don't suppose there is anything we can do about it.

If the bonds still haven't arrived you can check up on them at the following address. Army War Bond Office, 336 West Adams St., Chicago, Illinois.

I'm well and happy, particularly since I received the promotion, so don't worry about me. The sun is shining and it's a swell day. Hope we have a lot more just like it.

Received a letter from a nurse that I used to date when I was at Camp Edwards. She's in Australia. Hadn't heard from her for several months. Sure was a surprise. I'd lost her address so I wasn't able to write to her. It took almost two months for the letter to get here.

Had a letter from Dad. He's at Vancouver, Washington. He doesn't seem to like it there and thinks that he will go to San Francisco. Probably be a good thing for him. I have MaryLee's address, but I don't know when her birthday is. She writes to me about once a month.

About the Christmas gifts I want you to purchase and send for me. I'll send the money order back to you and I want you to use whatever additional money from the bank that is necessary. Send Jean something nice for her house. The sort of thing that she probably wouldn't get for herself. Use your own judgment and spend up to ten dollars. Give Dor a ten and tell her that I want her and Don to spend it in Billings. You know, dinner and dancing and drinking and whatever they like. If you don't think that ten will do it, use more. I don't know how prices are anymore. Get Donnie a good leather billfold. Like the one Dad gave me a couple of years ago. Send Dad a few good ties. Send some small thing to each of the San Francisco Rogers. Better send Frank some ties too. Send Bettie and Jean each a two ounce bottle of perfume. Pay about five dollars an ounce for it. I'll have to leave the choice of scent up to you. Bettie is Scotch, so try to get something like heather. The sales girl will probably be helpful. Get Jean a flowery perfume. Gardenia or something.

Now, about your gift. I would like to surprise you, because I know exactly what I want to give you, but that is impossible. Pay close attention, because I want your gift to be exactly so and no otherwise. Get a fitted over-night case. It must be leather and it must be good leather. Tuf-raw or tanned saddle cowhide. As I remember prices, you'll have to pay about thirty-five or forty dollars for it and no arguments. When I come home I am going to want to see it and if you didn't do as I told you, then we are going to have a big argument. I realize that I am spending more than I really should this year, but you do as I say. The raise that went with my promotion will cover it in six months time. I have enough money owed to me right now to pay for all of it and as soon as they pay me, I'll send it on to you. Maybe I'll get lucky in another crap game, in which case I'll have more money than I will know how to spend. Took the boys for eighty dollars in about thirty minutes, a few days ago.

Will have to close now. Don't work too hard and remember that I love you. I'll be home for next Christmas.

> Love,
> Bill

October 21, 1943

Dear Jeanne,

Am stealing the time to write this letter, so it probably won't be very long. And where, pray, did you think I was? Having a wonderful time. Lots of excitement.

Have been promoted. First Lt. now. New job too. Bn. Intelligence Officer. Nice, no? I think that I will do a pretty good job.

Don't think that the Army took Don. Just as well. I don't recommend this kind of life for a person of his temperament. Could be I'm wrong, the Army certainly remolded me.

Will send you another little souvenir in a few days. Nicer than the last one, I think.

Must go now, duty calls.

> Love,
> Bill

A new censorship policy was announced by Fifth Army Headquarters. Men could now tell their families that they were in Italy. And, so long as they didn't mention cities and identifiable geographical characteristics, they could talk about their combat experiences too.

Oct. 21, 1943

Dear Mom,

Just finished one letter to you, but received another one from you today. Also got a ruling on censorship, so there is a lot more I can tell you. First, I'm in Italy. I rather imagine you knew that. Second, I have been in combat. And now I can say for sure, don't worry about me. Those Jerries don't come near tough enough to bother me. Course I was scared. I don't know anyone that wasn't. But boy, do I like the excitement. Don't like being strafed by air craft, but we didn't get too much of that. Mostly artillery. Once a Jerry patrol with a light machine gun had me cornered (they thought) on a bald hill, but I got away, picked up a few men and ran them out of the country. My heart was sure going ninety to the dozen while those bullets were going over my head, but I had managed to get behind a little hump of ground and he couldn't touch me. Can't understand where Jerry got his "superman" reputation. If you are just throwing ammunition around, he'll stand his ground, but when you start shooting him between the eyes every time he sticks his head up, he's as yellow as they make them. And boy does he hate our artillery and I don't know that I blame him. It's terrific. I've seen some of the places that our aircraft bombed before the invasion, and from now on when they report that they have destroyed a target, I'm a believer. Literally not one stone on top of another. Not a building or a cross-road or a railroad that wasn't completely destroyed. For a peace loving people, we're about the roughest when it comes to fighting. The Germans and the British say we're crazy. But it seems to get results.

Pay close attention, because this is important. The Army provides an allowance for a dependant mother, if certain conditions exist. Now, as you know, I don't want you working, and there is no reason why you should, because I can support you, particularly if I am entitled to this allowance. If I don't have it coming, then I don't want it, but if I am entitled to it, I'm certainly going to try to get

it. Now here are the conditions. First of all the Army
wants to know what amount of money it will take to
support you in a reasonable and proper manner. It will
vary through-out the country depending on the cost of
living. I should think that seventy to eighty dollars would
be right for Montana. That would include providing food,
clothing, cost of habitation (in your case the taxes and
up-keep on the little house and land), and recreation.
This is not a bare necessities allowance. Then they want
to know what your actual living expenses are. They
should run about the amount I mentioned above.
Understand you wouldn't be working and getting
anything from anyone else but me. That is if you lived
with Dor or Jean, I couldn't claim it. Now, having
determined a reasonable and proper amount, they want
to know how much of that is defrayed by all other
sources than me. That must include all income that you
get from the ranch. However you are allowed to deduct
any debts that are being paid out of that money. Not your
personal debts but those that are an incurrance of the
estate. For example, if you received a payment of $500 a
year on the ranch and a hundred of that has to be paid to
the Govt. on the mortgage, and if you make a hundred
dollar payment to Frank on his share, then your income
from that source is $300. That's for a year. Now if that is
your only income outside of what I send you, then it
amounts to $25 a month. Since this amount is less than
half of the amount considered reasonable and proper, I
am entitled to an allowance for a dependant mother. You
must quit work and live on what I send you for a few
months before I can put in for the allowance, because I
must truthfully certify that for a certain period prior to my
making application that the above mentioned conditions
were true. Waiting to quit work until the allowance starts
arriving won't do it. So here is what I want you to do.
Figure out what it will cost you to live in Billings. Figure
on a small apartment, the Army doesn't expect an officer's
wife or mother to have to live in a hall bedroom. I think
that about $75 will be right. Then figure out how much
your income from all outside sources will be while you
are living there. Understand that you are not to be

working and no one else (Don, for instance) is to be contributing to your support. If this income is less than half the amount that it will take you to live, then I can claim a dependency allowance. If you are not clear on this you might talk it over with the banker at Laurel. As I remember him, he was a pretty nice fellow and he could figure out your income for you. Now it's up to you. If you figure out that I have a legal claim and you want me to do it, then quit work, move into town and live on the money that I am sending each month. Notify me of the exact conditions and as soon as a reasonable time has elapsed, I will apply for and get the allowance. I've repeated myself and gone into a lot of unimportant detail, but that is because mail service is so slow that there isn't time for any correspondence on the subject.

Received notice from the Readers Digest that you had given me a two year subscription for Christmas. Thanks a lot. It's a grand magazine, and amazingly enough it seems to arrive even faster than the letter mail.

I'll tell you how messed up our mail is. Received four letters from you today. Three regular dated Aug. 17, Aug. 23 and Sept. 27 and a V-Mail dated Oct. 7. The letter in which you say that you expect to receive the slippers in about a week reached me a week after the slippers did. Wish you hadn't used a ration stamp. I didn't know you would have to or I would never have asked for them.

Don't remember which ones they were, but several of my letters to you were written in a fox-hole. Hard to concentrate. Those damn 88's certainly can distract a person's attention.

Guess I'd better quit now. I still have several letters to write.

All my love,
Bill

Meanwhile, VI Corps moved on and the 36th Division was placed under II Corps. Major General Geoffrey Keyes (General Walker's junior), commanding.

Oct. 25, 1943

Dear Mom,

Only time for a short note. Wanted to return the strip-prints. The stupid photo-finishing shop has given you part of mine and part of someone else's. Mine is the super XX. The other is panatomic. Send them back and see if you can't get mine. Check the negatives and see if they correspond with the pics. If they do, then send them back. The pics of mine that are missing include shots of the Blue Ridge mountains, an Arab riding a laden jackass and several shots of French officers. Also a shot of some tall slim cypress trees and there should be some of me with a nurse.

Received two letters from you. One dated the 13th and one the 20 of Sept. Odd mail service. Because of the mail coming at such erratic intervals, I can't tell what mail of mine you have received. See if you can't get me a 35mm camera second-hand if necessary.

I am beginning to replace a few of the things I lost. Have some socks but no underwear or wool clothes yet. Won't be long tho. Could use a Shick injector razor if you can find one. I had two but lost one with the rest of my things and the one I have isn't much good. I have quite a few blades.

Bought a couple of coral necklaces for Bettie and Jean and the damn string broke. I thought they were pretty so I'm going to restring them on booby-trap wire as soon as I have time.

I'm well and happy. Like my new job fine. Am enclosing my promotion and transfer papers. Put them in my 201 file for me. If you can find a place that sells them, I could use about six silver bars (1st Lt.). Send one of those self-polishing cloths (Glad-rag etc.), I want my brass shiny for that victory parade down Unter den Linden.

Will write more in a day or so. Must wash for supper now.

Love,
Bill

The "Unter den Linden" was a fashionable street in pre-war Berlin.

The Salerno landing had revealed weaknesses in staff and command positions. General Walker reclassified two captains and a major. Through replacement and reassignment there were several changes in command and executive positions in the 142nd at regimental level, as well as at battalion and company levels. Second Battalion's headquarters company commander Captain Willard H. Gill was replaced on September 25. On October 1, 1943, by order of General Clark, Colonel Forsythe was replaced by Colonel Lynch as 142nd Regimental Commander. Clark said Forsythe was too old. General Walker found no fault with Forsythe and was upset with Clark's irregular and arbitrary appointment.

29 October 1943

Dear Mom,

Your letter of August 30th just arrived with the money-order. I have indorsed it to you and am enclosing it. If you have drawn the money from the bank to buy Christmas presents, deposit it. If not, use it and whatever additional money you need.

Haven't much to say at the present time. Suggest you read Jack Belden's article in the Sept. 27th issue of Time magazine.

Alvin finally sent me a letter. He seems to think that he will be called in the next draft. I doubt it. He's in a defense industry as well as having a family. Hope they don't take him. This is no place for a family man.

I'm glad you don't worry about me. Then I don't have to worry about you worrying about me, if you get what I mean. Some of the boys' families harass them all the time. Wanting to know if they are all-right.

I'm getting along fine in my new job and am beginning to like it. Hope I get to hold it for a while. The way things are now, I may get a new one anytime.

Lauretta wrote to me, the first time I've had a letter from her. Don and Lee have been doing all the corresponding for the family. It was an old letter, but welcome none-the-less.

I think that I am actually putting on weight. Sure feel good and am in good spirits. Have sent a few little souvenirs. Hope they arrive in good shape. Have acquired a few clothes and now own more than the one suit of underwear, pants, shirt and socks I had been reduced to. Feel like a plutocrat. Bake me a pint of scotch into a fruit cake and see if you can send it to me.

                        All my love,
                        Bill

Jack Belden was a war correspondent for both *Time* and *LIFE* magazines. He made the Salerno landing with the 36th Division. His article in the September 27, 1943 issue of *Time* describes his landing under fire and his desperate race across the beach. He was subsequently seriously wounded, and while wounded, almost caught in a tank battle. From his description of the objective taken and the events he witnessed, he made the landing in company with 2nd Battalion's commanding officer, Lt. Colonel Sam Graham's party.

[V-Mail]

                                        Oct. 30, 1943
Dear Al,
    Hope they don't draft you. This is no place for a married man. If they do, don't worry about allotments. They frequently reach your wife before you get paid. The govt. pays a private $50. He can allot $22.00 of this to a wife and the govt. raises the ante another $28.00. I think there is an additional amount for each child, but I'm not sure. I'm trying to get an allotment for Mom. War news all seems to be good. We might make the final drive next spring and summer. Hope it's over that soon. I'm just a little homesick. Italy is a decided improvement over Africa but can't compare with the States. Expect it will be winter soon. Won't like that. Read Dorothy Sayers' "Mind of the Maker" and am reading "Begin Here." Amazing! Don't like her Lord Peter Who-dun-its. Heard from my

nurse in Australia. What a long range romance that is.
Give Jeanne my love and tell the boys hello.

> Regards,
> Bill

On November 5, 1943, the division moved from Pozzuoli to
an assembly area near Villa Volturno.

> November 7, 1943

Dear Mom,

Haven't much of anything to say, but since I haven't
written for some time, I thought I'd better let you know
that I was all right. The rains are letting up a little so
perhaps life will be a little more comfortable from now
on. It sure is miserable living in the field when it rains all
the time. Had a cold a couple of weeks ago but have
gotten over it now. Afraid to take a bath tho, for fear I'll
catch another one. After you have been dirty for a while,
you get so you don't mind it.

Mail has been coming here very slowly. Guess I'll get
another big batch all at once. Received the gloves OK,
and they are swell. Just exactly what I wanted. Don't
forget that a few pair of heavy knitted wool socks will
come in handy this coming winter.

Hope you are taking care of the Christmas gifts I
wanted you to send for me. I sent the money order home
some time ago. You should have it by now. I have plenty
of money on hand now. In fact I'll probably send some
home after while. I make nearly twenty dollars more a
month now, than I did. Cigarettes are pretty scarce now
so if you can send me a few cartons they will certainly be
appreciated. I'm lucky enough to be in a tent tonight, so
I'm writing this by flashlight, propped on one elbow in
my bedroll.

If this war lasts much longer, you won't know me
when I get home. I have a pretty respectable mustache
now, and I guess I'm a bit quieter than I was.

See if you can't talk Donnie into going to work in an
aircraft plant. If he won't finish school he might at least
be making those good wages.

I've seen some very interesting things over here. We're not fighting all the time by any means. One place I visited was the "Grotto of the Cumae Sibyl." I don't think you know of it, but one of the Edgar teachers that knows his Roman mythology can tell you about it. Also saw the town that bears the same name as that "pillar" in eastern Montana. Was a little disappointed. Have a huge amt. of post cards that I'll send as soon as we are allowed to do so.

Haven't heard from Dad since he first moved to Vancouver. Guess he's all right tho.

Russia is certainly doing a wonderful job on the Eastern Front and we aren't doing so bad. I rather think that by the time you receive this that something will have broken on the North Sea, Norway or Finland or even in France. When that happens the end is in sight. Must close now.

All my love,
Bill

The "pillar" Bill mentioned as being in eastern Montana is "Pompay's Pillar," about thirty-five miles east of Billings on U.S. 10. Montana may have chosen to spell it differently, but Bill had been to visit the famous ruins of the city of Pompeii near Naples.

The reference to the "Grotto of the Cumae Sibyl" and Roman mythology concerns Virgil's *The Aeneid*, reputed to be one of the greatest of Latin poems. It tells the story of Aeneas and his travels from Carthage to the west coast of Italy where he had been told to seek the cave of the Sibyl of Cumae, a woman of deep wisdom. She takes him down to the World of the Dead. Bill had been visiting the ancient city of Cumae, about twelve miles west of Naples.

And he managed to take some pictures despite the stolen camera. Wood Jenkins, in an August 1990 letter, remembers:

When we landed at Salerno, my camera was salvaged, but I had no film. Bill lost his camera but saved his film. After Naples fell, Bill had a weekend in Naples. He borrowed my camera and used [his] film.

After going through Army hospitals in Italy, Oran, N. Africa and while in the hospital in U.S. I received my personal belongings. One item was the exposed negatives of the film Bill took in Naples. If I still have it I'll send it to you.

Unfortunately, Wood hasn't located the film yet and now fears it may have been lost in his many moves over the years.

November 8, 1943

Dear Jeanne,

Just received your V-Mail dated Oct. 23. Haven't much to say, but wanted to let you know that I am still O.K. Show the Postmaster this letter: "Dear Mr. P.M.: I hereby request my sister, Mrs. Alvin Shaffer, to send me some socks, wool, knitted, heavy, non G.I." (size 9 1/2).

Glad that rationing has eased up some-what. Hope it's all gone by the time I get home. I've had all of it that I want for a life time or two.

Here are the lyrics—good luck with the music.

I
The valiant line that held at Valley Forge
and subdued the western plain
rose again to meet our country's foe
in far off Alsace-Lorraine

chorus

Queen of battles, crowned with glory,
loud our praise to thee
'tween our home and foreign tyrant
stand the infantry

II
Thru the bloody pass at Kasserine
and the hell of El-Guettar
it was bayonets that cleared the way
for America's bright star

(repeat chorus)

In the final battle of the Earth
on Armageddon's plain
You can bet your roll, the infantry
will save the day again

repeat chorus

Hope you like it!

Cpl. Stimson, our battalion clerk, is sitting near me, looking at his girl's picture with a large magnifying glass. And I sadly fear that it is her legs he is gazing at with such studied intensity. Alas—what will become of the younger generation?

I wrote Mom, asking her to take care of my Christmas presents for me. Hope that they arrive on time.

How about a picture of you and the "boys." I lost the family snap-shot I had.

Must go now. Lots of luck and

Love
Bill

Charles W. Stimson Jr.
(1942)

Nov. 11, 1943

Dear Mom,

Guess I have forgotten to write for a few days. I try to
write twice a week when I can. Haven't received much
mail lately, but we are getting so much mail tonight that
the mail orderly can't carry it and we had to send a jeep,
so I should get a lot.

AS I WAS

They just passed out the mail and I only received two
letters. One from Bettie and one from a Lt. in Sicily.
Phooey!

I'm still O.K. and having a grand time. Liking my new
job fine. It gives me a lot of freedom, as I don't have any
men to worry about. Running a platoon is darn near like
raising a family.

Have visited a lot of interesting places here in Italy.
Guess I told you I had been in combat. It isn't nearly as
bad as I expected it to be. There is very little hand to
hand fighting, mostly artillery and you don't have to
worry about it if you have a good fox hole. I didn't use
mine much. There was too much fun to be had. Patrols
are awful exciting, cause you're on your own, I guess.

The time I had my biggest scare, I wasn't in danger at
all, I just thought I was. Our outfit was holding one end of
a ridge line along which ran a pretty good gravel road.
There was supposed to be another outfit on the other end
of the ridge, but no one seemed to know whether they
had been able to take their sector or not. So I got a driver
that had lots of guts and I armed myself with a bazooka
and off we went. We traveled about 10 miles an hour so
that we could get a good look at the area ahead of us.
The driver was watching the left and I took care of the
other side. We traveled this way for a couple of miles and
didn't run across anything and I guess I got a little
careless. As I was looking off to the right, we rounded a
sharp turn and I felt the jeep stop suddenly. I turned
around to see what was the matter and the driver
couldn't even talk, he just pointed ahead of us. I looked,
and there, not thirty yards away, a Mark IV tank was

sitting right in the middle of the road. I was so darn scared I couldn't move and the two of us darn fools just sat there and looked at it. After a few minutes we got over it and as it hadn't showed any signs of life we walked up and looked it over. There wasn't a thing wrong with it. It had just run out of gas and been abandoned. Sometimes yet, when I think about rounding that corner, the cold chills run up my back.

Looks as though Russia were going to win this war. She ought to be in Berlin by spring. Rommel is a pretty tricky customer but this Von [Vietinghoff] doesn't seem to be much on anything but defense.

Haven't heard from Dad since that first letter from Vancouver. Guess he's all right. Bettie's letter was dated the 25th of Oct. and she hadn't heard from her younger brother Bob for over a month. He's in a Ranger outfit and has undoubtedly gone overseas.

Jeanne writes more often than she used to but just the usual chit-chat. I like the long letters you write better.

Don't forget that I need a 35mm camera if you can get one. It will probably have to be bought from a second hand outfit in the east. The firms all advertise in Popular Photography! Time for supper now.

All my love,
Bill

The Allies had given themselves a very tough job in Italy. The American army was trying to fight its way north from Naples along an ancient Roman highway, the Via Casilina, through the Italian interior to Rome and beyond. German strategy called for a slow withdrawal to the north, falling back to a series of fortified lines which took full advantage of the natural defensive positions provided by the Italian mountains. The slow withdrawal allowed time for further fortification of the lines. The "Bernhard Line" crossed the Italian peninsula at its narrowest place, just north of Naples. Behind it was the "Gustav Line" with Monte Cassino and the Rapido River. The defensive action was effectively carried out by General Von Vietinghoff.

Via Casilina at Mignand turnoff, 1943 above, 1991 below.

Via Casilina (Hwy 6) looking towards Cassino, note the abbey. 1991. The mountain in the background is Mt. Lungo.

View from
Mt. Lungo of
intersection
of mountain
road from
Venafro and
San Pietro
with
Highway 6.

On November the 15th, having assimilated its replace-
ments, been inspected, and found ready for action again, the
142nd Regiment went back into the line relieving the 3rd
Division's 7th Infantry. This was at the German Bernhard Line
in the mountains controlling the Mignano Gap. The Mignano
Gap is an opening in the mountains through which runs the
Via Casilina, and which is the gateway to the Liri valley,
Cassino, and Rome. It was cold and it rained continuously.
Lt. Rogers kept busy in his new job.

Former Staff Sergeant Mabene J. Allen, in a February 1990
letter, recalls Lt. Rogers and gives a job description:

> I knew Buck personally. I was in the same
> Headquarters and had dealings with him every day.
> He was in S II section and I was in S III section. I was
> plans and training and he had charge of Battalion
> Intelligence section. He stayed up and beyond our
> front lines scouting out the enemy, calling back for
> fire power, and telling us what the enemy was and
> their location. He was the type of officer that would
> go far beyond the call of duty ... If it hadn't been
> for his forward observing we would have lost lots
> more men.

But it is the nature of war that men would still be lost and
wounded. On November 16, 1943, the day after 2nd Battalion
re-entered the line, at about 2:30 p.m., Bill's friend Charles
W. Stimson, Battalion Clerk, was nearly killed by German
artillery. While he was never to see Lt. Rogers again, Charles hasn't forgotten his friend. Forty-seven years later he
writes:

> Yes, I am the Charles Stimson that was a friend of
> William A. (Buck) Rogers ... Roger, I would like to
> think that Buck and I were good friends. He joined our
> unit a long time before we went overseas ... Buck was
> not far from me when I was hit ... I spent months in
> hospitals in Italy and Africa ... Buck was a good man
> and a darn good soldier.

142 RCT JOURNAL for 17 Nov. 1943:

"1140   Lt Rogers 2nd Bn. reported: estimated
platoon of enemy at 965115. Hqs. Co. fired
mortars on position at 1200 . . .

"1500   Lt Rogers, 2nd Bn. talked to Capt. Simpson
at 1430: column of 14 Germans moving south
at 962113. Put mortars on, and dispersed
them. One, heavily loaded, ran away . . .

"19 November 1943 . . .

"7 P   Lt Rogers: British FO with Co. E. He observed
some men digging something out of ground.
Carrying it on their head to house. 1700 at
969121. At extreme distance (940120)
observed column of trucks approaching with
lights on (late at night) NW up valley. Trucks
put on blackout lights at rise, stopped near
house . . .

"9 P   Lt Rogers reported that Arty OP picked up
Inf in open at 974125. Could see shelter
halves. He was told by Captain Simpson not
to fire in that sector . . .

"10 P   Lt Rogers (Vic 955120) counted 17 men. OP
operator at Co G receiving sniper fire . . .

"12 P   Lt Rogers: MG firing from 965109. Trucks
previously reported were seen in NE corner
of coordinate square 940120 . . .

"25 P   Lt Col Lynch talked to Lt Rogers, S-2 2nd Bn;
15 prisoners being sent back—captured at
964109 . . .

"27 P   Capt Simpson talked to Lt Rogers; 2nd Bn in
fire fight, sending 21 captured Germans
back. No casualties in 2nd Bn.

"21 Nov 1943...

"33 P Lt Rogers reported that patrol under Lt. Johnson, Co E, that observed Arty barrage and reports: Gone #6 on group of house-all hit well, #7 at stream got hit very lightly: #6 could not reach on account of enemy mortar and small arms...

"50 P Capt Simpson told Lt Rogers: Boundary limits for tomorrow (only) patrolling 968113 NE to 974124...

"54 P Lt Rogers: No report from patrol.

"55 P Lt Rogers: Checked with Co F—radio not working...

"22 Nov 1943...

"5 P Lt Rogers: No. 1 patrol went out 500 yards. Contacted friendly troops on right and left but no enemy. Returned at 0900...

"31 P Lt Rogers: Daytime patrol left 0830—NW to patrol limiting line. American soldier body at 972116. Woman's body 200 yds N of that point. Patrol Ldr and 1 man advanced to within 100 yds of group of houses at 970118, believed to be vacant at 1000 heard MG firing coming from extreme left ridge. No wires, mines or booby traps in vicinity 972116. Trees have been felled across. draw at that point. There is wire near woman's body. Returned at 1230...

"23 Nov 1943...

"7 P Lt Rogers: No further report from patrol, will make complete report later...

"28 P Lt. Rogers: New relief in position at 1545."

Nov. 23, 1943

Dear Mom,

Have received quite a bit of mail recently, but haven't had a minute to answer any of it.

The Christmas packages have already begun to arrive and of course we open them right away. Don and Lauretta sent a box of cigars and Jean and Bettie sent me some "pocket books" and a beautiful silver identification bracelet. Guess the rest of the packages will arrive long before Christmas, but that's alright.

Can't feel very upset about Art and Jeannette. Still can't understand why Donnie doesn't get a good job in a war industry. By the way, what outfit is Warren Patterson in? If you want some battle stories, I've got plenty of them, but I'd rather not write about them unless you want me to.

The rains continue and I have a cold that has become so much a part of me that I'd feel lonesome without it.

Hope the winter isn't too cold out there. And I hope that by this time that you have moved into Billings and are living on the money that I send home.

Jeanne writes occasionally and I actually received a letter from Dorothy. Haven't heard from Dad since he arrived in Vancouver. Guess he'll write when he feels like it. Lauretta writes once in a while.

I'm living in a grist-mill right now. One of the old kind run by a water wheel, and all the little natives bring their wheat and corn to have it ground.

We finally got some magazines and read and saw pictures of some of the fighting we have been in. There was so much excitement at the time that we didn't get a chance to take a good look.

Will write more when I have more time.

Love,
Bill

The October 25, 1943 issue of *LIFE* carried pictures of the landing at Salerno, including an offshore view of the tower at Paestum.

The landing on Green beach. Note the Paestum tower at right.

Green beach and the Paestum tower, 1991.

Aerial view of the Paestum landing area with the Tower of Paestum in the foreground and Mt. Soprano rising from the plain in the background. The creek separates Green and Yellow beaches.

24 Nov 43
Italy

Dear Jeanne,

Have a few minutes so I'll try to catch up on my correspondence. Have two V-Mails from you, both October.

Christmas packages have started to arrive. A box of good cigars from uncle Don and a beautiful heavy silver identification bracelet from Bettie and Jean.

A letter from Dorothy the other day, the second since I've been overseas. Uncle Frank stopped there a few days on his way to San Diego. Her boy is apparently a world beater. Art and Jeannette have split up and will probably get a divorce.

Mom seems to be all right. She seems to get into town once in a while. I'm trying to get her to move into Billings and live on the money that I send home. I haven't heard from Dad for over six weeks. Lee Rogers starts U of C in March. Can't imagine her being that grown up.

I'm not supposed to write on the back [side of the note paper], but if the base censor were where I am, I think he would do the same. The only things I have with me are what I can carry on my back, and when this little tablet is finished, there is no more.

Do you suppose you could get me a couple of sets of 1st Lt. bars. And don't forget to knit me some heavy socks (9 1/2). Already I feel the cold. Bettie has just finished a Nurses Aide course and works at Redford Receiving. Jean is taking a Dietitians Aide course.

How are the little fellows? Roger (I guess I mean Roger) must be a pretty good sized kid now. Tell them hello for me and give my regards to Al.

Love,
Bill

(Author's note: what a thrill it was to see my Uncle Bill make a reference to me.)

142nd RTC JOURNAL for 24 Nov 1943:

"24 P   Lt. Rogers: Patrol left at 0900. Went along
                 creek to houses. Did not find mines or
                 boobytraps. Single strand of wire along
                 standing trees . . .

"28 P   Lt. Rogers: Combat outpost is established at
                 position 984114. Last contact with Rondo
                 was at 976124 yesterday. Patrols of last night
                 and morning found no one there."

On November 25, Thanksgiving day, General Walker ex-
pressed his concern that the men were developing trench foot
because they were not able to dry their feet for days at a time.

142nd RCT JOURNAL for 26 Nov 1943:

"7 P   Lt Rogers, OP at 963099 reports: 7 wounded,
                 2 killed in Co F; our planes strafed enemy. At
                 1100, after phosphorus shell landed on ridge,
                 a German police dog came down toward
                 our line. No enemy activity seen . . .

"27 Nov 1943 . . .

"16 P   Lt Rogers called: at 1645 4 men observed
                 moving west 958083. (Probably) . . .

"28 Nov 1943 . . .

" P   Fr. Lt. Rogers: OP referred to in last nights
                 report was on Mt. Camino. Also reported
                 small column of smoke coming from among
                 rocks in saddle North of Mt. Camino. Arty.
                 Air-burst over this position."

On December 3 the 142nd attacked and captured Mt. La
Difensa and Mt. Maggiore as part of General Walker's plan.
They had to go through mud and water, soaked to the skin and
muddied from head to foot. Supply was a constant problem in
the mountain fighting. At night it took a man eight hours to go

the five miles from where the jeep could go no further. Mule pack trains would be organized later. General Walker felt that few Americans have ever had to fight under more difficult conditions.

In spite of the adverse conditions, 2nd Battalion advanced rapidly. By the end of the day on December 4, all objectives assigned to the 142 had been taken.

142nd RCT JOURNAL for 3 Dec 1943:

"26 P   Lt Rogers: Messenger from White 6 says Bn on 596 . . .

"5 Dec 1943 . . .

" P   Lt Rogers reports he is established in an OP in the NW edge of Co E area, overlooking the valley to the NE, N, and NW. Msg was relayed through Rotate White."

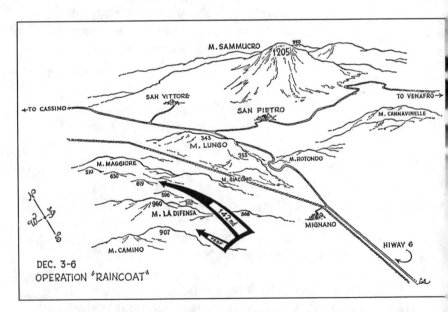

Attack on Camino hill mass by 142nd Inf Regt and First Special Service Force, December 3-6, 1943.

On December the 5th an attempt was made to supply the 142nd by air, from an A-36 fighter bomber. They only managed to get one package of rations from three plane drops.

During the night of December 5 the Germans counterattacked in force against 2nd Battalion's "E" Company. Mid-afternoon on December 6, "E" company was attacked again. At 1625 on the 7th, the 2nd Battalion was counterattacked. While that was repulsed in about an hour, at 0700 on the 8th they were still engaged with the enemy. Enemy shelling was continuous. This was very tough fighting. By December the 10th however, battalion patrols reported no enemy activity. During the night of December the 12th, the 2nd Battalion was relieved and moved into the valley.

IX
An Earned Rest

Dear Mom,

I haven't been able to write to you for a long time so I'll try to make up for it now with a real big letter.

I'm at a rest camp. Nothing wrong with me, just worn out. It's a swell place. A grand hotel in a famous town, where all we have to do is relax. Our outfit sends one officer a week, and this week it was my turn.

I have five letters from you and am going to try to answer all of them now. I'm sharing a room with a Lt. Hearn. He's a grand guy. He's a liaison officer from the Artillery on duty with our Bn. Just before we went into the lines the last time, he gave the officers of our Bn. a short course in directing artillery fire, then while we were in combat, his forward observer was shot out of his observation post (about 50 ft. from mine) during a counter attack, so I directed the artillery fire for almost two days. Guess I did a pretty good job, cause I've sure been complimented.

The cigarettes you sent me arrived just in time to come here with me, and they are certainly welcome. Our cigarette supply is rationed and I was getting awfully low. Wish I could have seen Jack Estes when he was home. Haven't heard from Chris yet but I guess I will soon. I don't know the girl that Orville McCabee married. I thought he had been drafted. Thanx a lot for the pictures of you with the horse. They are swell.

You certainly worked hard on the little house. It must look grand. I doubt that Jeanne will want to stay there however. She never felt very much at home in Montana.

I think I told you that the gloves had arrived and they were certainly a god-send, but I have worn them to shreds on the rocks. We were fighting in the mtns. You might try to send me another pair. You should be able to get a pair of leather roping gloves at the Penny store or Vaughn-Ragsdale in Laurel.

I'd like to tell you more about the war but I can't tell you anything important without naming places and dates and such and we're not allowed to do that. I'll tell you all about it when I get home. Once we went for four days on three chocolate bars and a concentrated "K" meal and the only water we had was what we could drink out of hollows in the rock. It rains all the time. After a while they dropped food from airplanes, but they dropped just as much of it on Jerry's side as on ours and then we had to fight for it. I've had several narrow escapes, men killed all around me and I wasn't touched, so I guess I'll get thru this thing all right. I've been caught in two counter-attacks. One of them drove our infantry off the hill and left me and two other fellows surrounded, but we crawled on our bellies in the mud for eight hundred yards and got away all right. Next day we counter-attacked and took the hill back.

If you need any of my money for the house or anything else, go ahead and use it. That's what it's for. Glad that you wrote about the bonds. I received the flex-stone and the map and they are just exactly what I wanted. Glad that you got the watch. It will probably be waiting for me when I get back to my outfit. Received Jeanne's package and will write and thank her as soon as I can. She had included a pocket chess set, which pleased me muchly. I get a hundred and eighty-five dollars a month now. This money doesn't mean much. After my allotment is taken out and insurance etc. I get fifty to spend and that's plenty. About renting the land. If you do, make them put up the bldgs. and have the ownership of them revert to you whenever they fail to pay or decide to quit. Don't invest your money in their scheme. Wish I could go deer hunting this year. Some venison would taste good.

Hope you have decided to quit work. It's just a habit. After I come home you can keep house for me and we'll have a lot of fun travelling. I sure know how to get around now. Wish you could see some of the places I've been. The hotel I'm staying in now catered to the very rich in pre-war times. The King of Sweden once stayed here. Am going to try to go to the opera Sunday. They are playing La Boheme in the opera house where Caruso used to sing. Not sure that I can get tickets.

Had my teeth cleaned when I first got here and before I could get out of the chair, he had four fillings in. Just little ones. Did I ever mention Dr. Epstein? He was our asst. Bn. Surgeon. He was hit (not bad) in one of our last operations.

Lt. Hearn and I spend most of our time eating and sleeping. We walk around a couple of hours each day (me with the aid of a cane, my feet are pretty beat up). We were pretty sick when we first got here (our stomachs had shrunk up from eating concentrated rations) but we are all right now. We'll be raring to go when our week is up.

Will write some more tomorrow or Sunday.

All my love
Bill

The rest camp where Bill and Lt. Charles L. Hearn were staying was the Hotel Vittoria in Sorrento, Italy. The Vittoria was a rest center for officers of the Fifth Army from October 1943 until 1945. In a November 1990 letter to the author, Charles Hearn recalled:

Yes, I ... roomed with ... "Buck" Rogers in Sorrento Italy. We could look across the Bay of Naples to the north and see Naples and Mt. Vesuvius.

Charles Hearn, 1993

We went across the straits to the west to the Isle of Capri while we were there. We stayed there in Sorrento for a whole week! We had been in some <u>very</u> severe fighting prior to our going to Sorrento for a week of R & R. I remember that I had not had my clothes off for <u>6 weeks</u> just prior to going to the Rest Camp. We had been on field rations all this time and the food where Lt. Rogers and I stayed was wonderful!

Charles Hearn, Roger Shaffer at "Green beach," September 9, 1993.

On December 22, 1943, the 142 Regiment moved to an assembly area in the vicinity of Venafro, Italy. Venafro is a small Italian town situated in the upper Volturno River valley amidst grainfields and vineyards.

Venafro, 1943

Venafro, 1991

[V–Mail]

22 December 43

Dear Mom,
     I wrote you a long letter a couple of days ago. I've just
finished a week at a rest camp. Was in pretty bad shape,
but feel fine now. Wish I could tell you where I am. It's
beautiful here. Must be gorgeous in the spring. Haven't
received any mail while I have been down here, so I
suppose I have a lot waiting for me. Hope you were able
to take care of my Christmas shopping for me. No telling
how long this thing is going to go on. Can't see less than
six months or a year over here. Would like to see you
again. Tell everyone hello for me. Had a letter from Dad
saying Don was with him. Wish the kid would settle
down in one place long enough to get some schooling.
Write when you can and tell me all the news.

Love and Merry Christmas,
Bill

During the afternoon of Christmas Day, General Clark
visited the 142nd. He awarded a Distinguished Service Cross
to Sergeant Manuel S. Gonzales, pinned new eagles on
"Colonel" Lynch and new First Lieutenant's bars on Evan
MacIlraith. Evan also had some luck that evening at poker, as
we see by Bill's next letter.
     On December 26 the 142nd Regiment was ordered to
relieve the 504th Parachute Regiment in the Mt. Sammucro
sector. Second Battalion Clerk Roy E. Caudill's log entry for
26 December 1943:

1.   Received word at 2030 that Col. Graham,
            Capt. Armstrong, Lt. Rogers, and Sgt. Allen
            leave on reconnaissance.

27 December 43

Dear Mom,

Returned a few days ago from the rest camp and am
feeling fine again. Christmas was a pretty quiet affair.
Played poker Christmas night and made fifty dollars and
MacIlraith won a lot and paid me the sixty he owed me,
so I'm affluent again. Weather here is still miserable but
is getting colder, so perhaps the mud will freeze up and
the damnable rain will turn to snow. We have
combat-suits now and they are warm. Forgot to enclose
the transfer papers but it doesn't matter. Thanx for taking
care of my Christmas shopping. The gifts you picked out
sounded all right to me. The case you get for yourself had
better be a good one.

I received the billfold from Donnie and will write and
thank him. It's a swell one. Has a lot of transparent
pockets and I filled them with pictures. Have a new one
of Bettie in her Nurses Aide Uniform.

You've put so much work on the place it must look
like a picture house. I'm glad you want to quit work. Now
we'll have to straighten out the details. You sent me an
itemized expense sheet which certainly indicates the
need for an allotment. The important thing now is, will
your income from all other sources than me exceed
$40.00, that being about half of what it will take to
support you? If it does not, then quit work and begin to
live on my money and let me know as soon as possible. If
it does exceed the $40 (a few dollars needn't matter) then
I can't get the allotment and you will have to keep on
without it.

Yes I had turkey on Thanksgiving. Had it for breakfast
and didn't get another meal for about thirty-six hours.
Christmas was a lot better. Glad that you hear from Frank
so often. We'll go take a look at Arizona after I get home.
Sure hope the sox arrive before long. It's getting a little
chilly.

Was just told that I have to go on a reconnaissance
tomorrow. Damn! I am only a few miles from my old outfit
and wanted to get over to see them. Saw one of the Lts.
that gave me my recruit training at Ft. Lewis—He was at
the rest camp when I was. He's a Major now.

Received my first copy of R.D. Thanks again. It's going to be nice having that coming each month. Jean Boyle is going to send me the overseas edition of the New Yorker.

Received another letter from my African friend, Sgt. Meghelli, written in English this time. He's with the Free French under General La Cluc now. He wrote from Rabet, but there is no telling where he is now. No letters from Bob Cromwell. Think he may have gone to England.

Have a hunch that Bettie's younger brother is over here. If he is I'll have to look him up.

I've about run out of anything to say. Lots of luck— Happy New Year and all that stuff. Say hello to everyone for me.

> Love,
> Bill

Relief of the 504th Parachute Regiment was completed by the 29th of December. The Battalion was in a defensive position, and action thereafter consisted mainly of patrols to maintain contact with the enemy. The wind blew and it snowed.

142nd RCT JOURNAL for 3 Jan 1944:

" P   Lt Rogers: 6 Germans with Red Cross flag, unarmed moving west from 942207. Saw them personally...

" P   Lt. Rogers reported 4 Germans, 2 pack mules on trail via 960205 moving E. at 1430. He was directed to observe for gun firing on 2nd Bn. Rogers reported only single rounds coming in.

"5 Jan 1944...

"11 P   Lt Rogers rptd 10 P-51s strafed 2nd & 3rd bn areas. Speedy 2 notified of strafing...

" P   Lt Rogers rptd—1600 German comd car left CERVARO. Turned N toward CASSINO. 1625

> on trail via 955211 4 German medics
> walking E passed 8 Germans moving W.
> carrying litter.

"7 Jan 1944 Ceppagna, Italy...

"9 P   Lt Rogers reptd—can count 40 friendly tanks
near base of MT PORCHIA. Some moving.
Can see friendly troops approaching base of
MT CHIAIA apparently unopposed. No
enemy activity now. Many troops in SAN
VITTORE. Some S/A fire early this morning
to extreme right in front of SABOTAGE.

. . .

" P   Lt Rogers reptd enemy on HILL 850 and
friendly troops advancing up ridge toward
850...

"17 P   Lt Rogers from WHIT OP reported definitely
identifying 12 Germans taking positions on
Hill 850."

During the night of January 7, Second Battalion received
orders to withdraw. By the 8th, the entire regiment was in the
rest and training area in the vicinity of Alife.

January 1944

Dear Mom,

It has been a long time since I last wrote and even
longer since I last had a letter from you. I hope that you
are all-right. I'm as chipper as a young colt. Have had
several days rest and am almost back to normal. Climbing
these mountains certainly takes the starch out of me. A
few days rest, a few good hot meals and I'm rar'ing to go
again. Hope we stay out long enough for me to get caught
up on my correspondence. People will begin to think that
I've forgotten them.

The watch finally arrived. We seem to have very good
luck with our packages. As far as I know, they have all

gotten through. The watch is a good one and certainly
worth the money as hard as they are to get. The package
from Dorothy containing the steel wool, milk and fruit
arrived the same day. Tell her thanks, for me. I may not
have time to write her a separate letter.

We made an attack some time ago and after we had
taken our objective they weren't able to supply us, so we
had to live for four days on two concentrated chocolate
bars, four ounces of cheese, eight tiny crackers and a
stick of chewing gum. It rained constantly, so we had
plenty of water, although it was pretty muddy. I lived
with my Sgt. (we live, fight and even sleep in pairs, so
that one man out of two is always awake in case of a
counter-attack) and all we talked about for the four whole
days was food. I know how his mother makes chocolate
cake with coffee icing and served it with whipped cream
(he eats whipped cream on everything) and he knows
exactly how you make strawberry shortcake with biscuit
instead of cake dough and how to bake sour-dough
biscuits and flap-jacks.

Had a letter from Frank with several pictures in it.
He's looking well. Wish I had a pocket full of that Arizona
sunshine to carry around and take out and look at once in
a while. Sunny Italy my eye.

The mail orderly just brought me a swell, long letter
from you and one from Bettie. Think I'll ask her again, to
marry me sometime after the war.

In your letter you still seem confused as to my duties
so I'll try to explain them. While an attack is being made,
my section and I move with the Command Post (CP) group
generally just in rear of the assault elements. As soon as
the objective is taken I take one man with me and go
forward on a reconnaissance of the front lines and pick a
location for an observation post. Then I send the man
back to bring up the rest of the group. While he's gone I
look over the enemy dead to see what outfit they
belonged to and learn what I can from their defense
positions and weapons. When the men arrive we set up
the OP. We usually set up right in the front lines and
once, in order to get a more advantageous position, I set
up in front of the lines. Was cut off from our troops by a

counter attack and haven't tried it again. We watch the
enemy positions, with the aid of a powerful scope and
make reports as to the enemy dispositions, locations,
weapons etc. When prisoners are captured, I question
them (I have an interpreter) if it is convenient or just send
them on to the rear. Once when we were short of an
artillery observer (the arty OP was about sixty feet from
mine and one of them was shot with a machine pistol
and his replacement was captured) I directed arty fire for
four days. That's a lot of fun. Now that I have it down on
paper it doesn't sound like much but it seems to keep us
busy in actual practice.

The little house is certainly going to look fine. You're
putting a lot of work on it. I guess you have decided by
now whether or not you are entitled to the dependency
allotment I wrote about. If you want it, we'll put your
requirements as eighty dollars a month. Let me know
how much your income is from all other sources than me
and when you first started to live on what I send, as I
explained it in that other letter and I'll put in for the
allotment. I figure that after the war I'll get my store
started and we can have a nice apartment in town during
the winter and during the summer we can live at the
little house. Or at least you can and I'll spend as much
time there as I can.

The letter that just came was written Dec. 5 and had
the clipping about the silver dollars.

I'm getting awfully proud of this Battalion of mine.
We've been given some pretty tough jobs and come out
on top. We've taken every objective we've been given
and we've never broken under a counter-attack yet. Had
a company give ground one night (the time my OP was
cut off) but the Bn. held and the next day the company
rallied and re-took the hill. Not very many of the old
familiar faces around any more, but the number killed is
amazingly small.

Had a letter from Bob Cromwell a few days ago.
Seems to be living the life of Riley. Said that he had seen
Col. Goddard. I'd sure like to see him again.

Played poker last night till eleven and wound up
even. I have become a fair player and usually manage to

come out ahead. Before I had been in combat I wouldn't play anything but nickels and dimes. How a little war can change a man. Best pot I've ever won was sixty dollars and that's not hay.

Dinner's ready now and I can't think of anything more to write anyway, so good bye for now.

All my love,
Bill

Former 2nd Battalion Messenger Johnnie A. Pricer remembered "the walking arsenal Lt. Buck Rogers" and his job:

Johnnie Pricer

... several of the officers and I were standing in a bunch talking to him and he kept us all laughing. He was a walking arsenal—one 45 sub, one 9mm German machine folding handle gun, one M-1 Carbine, one M-1 30 cal rifle, one 45 auto, one 9mm Walther P-38, 2 bowie knives, ammo for all plus half a dozen grenades on his belt. They ask him how he could walk with all that. He laughed it off and said "in my position you have to be prepared."

Johnnie went on to explain that once Bill set up in the front lines (or occasionally ahead of the front line), he positioned the weapons for fast use in the event his OP was attacked. His memory of Bill is a good one:

To know Lt. Rogers was to love him. And if he had an enemy it was on the other side ... I can see that little guy as plain as if I were looking at him in person—standing there all armed to the teeth—he was real funny with his humor. He'd weigh 120 or 130 lbs—but boy he was all there.

The first few days at Alife were devoted to improving the bivouac area and processing through the Fifth Army Sterilization Unit. The officers and men got hot showers and a complete issue of clean clothing.

While Bill found some time to write while at Alife, "rest and training" meant work too. After several days of "training" in mountain maneuvering, there were two days of river crossing practice.

142nd RCT JOURNAL for 15 Jan 1944 (River Crossing Problem):

"1815 [hours] Lt. Rogers reported in to await the orders of the 2nd Bn to move.

"2045   Colonel Lynch told Lt. Rogers to tell Lt. Col. Graham to move out.

"2115   Lt. Rogers called and reports that the 2nd Bn. has completed their leaving the assembly area."

Roy Caudill's log for 17 January 1944:

"Five NCO's, one from each Company and Lt. Rogers went out on billeting detail . . ."

20 January 1944 . . .

"Col. Graham, Company Commanders from each Company and S2 [Bill] and S3 leave on reconnaissance and returned when they had finished looking at their respective areas."

Impatient with the slow progress up the Italian peninsula, Winston Churchill wanted some decisive action. Specifically, a seaborne landing that would put troops behind the Gustav line. And so "Operation Shingle" developed. Briefly, Allied troops would bypass the Gustav line by making a landing at Anzio, some thirty-five miles south of Rome. At the same time Clark's Fifth Army would attack the Gustav line, drawing the enemy south, away from the Anzio landing. Then the Allies were to link up, catching the Germans between them. The landing at Anzio took place at 0200 on January 22, 1944. The American army's part of the coordinated attack on the Gustav line fell to the 36th Division.

But the early German strategy had changed. A determined stand was going to be made at the Gustav line. A natural defensive position anyway, Hitler had authorized extensive fortifications. The line had been reinforced with concrete, armored turrets, and antitank guns. The Rapido River was the main defensive barrier. The riverbanks and approaches were mined. The Germans had diverted the river flow and flooded the American side of the river. They cut the trees and brush to give them a clear field of fire. On the north side of the Rapido, German infantry was dug in. There was a line of machine gun posts with interlocking fire. Artillery fire guided by observation posts on the heights made a daylight approach impossible. The dominant feature of the Gustav line was the Abbey of Monte Cassino. It sat high on the mountain in perfect position to observe and control any Allied movement in the valley below. This was a textbook defensive position designed to withstand a concerted attack and inflict maximum punishment on the attackers.

In what is surely one of the most controversial military operations of World War II, the 141st and 143rd Regiments of the 36th Division were ordered to cross the Rapido River and attack into the teeth of the German main line of resistance. During the night of January 20 and again on the 21st, the two regiments made their crossing attempts. The attacks were a failure. Not even a dent had been made in the German defenses. It wasn't for lack of trying. The 143rd lost a total of 969 officers and men killed, wounded, and missing. The 141st lost 1,050. It was a slaughter. The losses were so high both regiments ceased to exist as fighting units. The 142nd Regiment had been held in Corps reserve in an assembly area near Mignano.

During the night of January 21-22, Second and Third Battalions of the 142nd Regiment were ordered to move to an assembly area southeast of Mt. Trocchio.

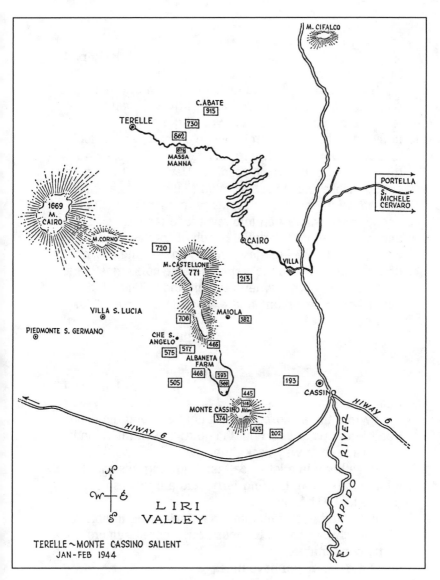

Terelle-Monte Cassino salient, January-February, 1944.

Roy Caudill's log for 21 January 1944:

"0900 Col. Graham, Capt. Armstrong, Lt. Rogers and Sgt. [Mabene] Allen to go to forward assembly area about 1 mile south of Trocchio."

[V-Mail]

21 January 44

Dear Jeanne and Al,

Have an un-answered letter from each of you, so this will have to serve for both. I'm healthy, well fed and reasonably happy. Once in a while I get a little home-sick, but would probably go crazy if I had to look at four walls very long. The rehabilitation of Rogers, after this war, is going to be a problem. Having a little fun and enough close calls to satisfy even Nietzsche. The socks arrived safely the other day. Many thanks. A bunch of people have just drifted into my abode (a fake hay-stack) and we are about to drink a bunch of cognac. A sort of celebration before "the lusty young go running down to die." Could you send me a small folding corkscrew? Sure could use one. Write when you can and tell me all the news. Love to everyone and a kick "em la derriere" for the boys.

Bill

21 January 44

Dear Dad,

I wrote the enclosed letter a hell of a long time ago. Don't know what I said but I'm going to send it along just to prove I wrote way back then.

Have been in a lot since then. Fighting this country is a lot tougher than fighting Jerry. Had a light case of trench-foot. O.K. now.

Am living in an imitation hay-stack. Used to hold a Jerry machine gunner. He doesn't live here anymore. Pretty comfortable.

Write when you have time.

Love,
Bill

In spite of the slaughter at the Rapido and the loss of two infantry regiments already, General Keyes, II Corps Commanding General, was still willing to throw more men into an impossible situation. He returned the 142nd Regiment to 36th Division control and ordered Walker to have them make yet a third attack the morning of the 23rd. Fortunately, while the 142nd was still making attack preparations, the order was rescinded. Bill managed to work in another letter. It was to be his last.

23 January 44

Dear Mom,

    Still nothing to write about, but I have some spare time and I don't know how much I'll have in the future.

    Had a nice letter from Bettie and Jean thanking me for the perfume. They seemed to like the gifts so I guess you did a nice job of selecting them. Thanks a lot.

    Still no word from you on how large an income you have. Wish you'd let me know and also tell me when you started living on my allotment. That is, the date you quit working. Need this info in order to apply for the allotment.

    Am feeling pretty good and have completely recovered from my case of trench-foot. Stomach is OK again, so I haven't a complaint in the world. My luck is holding pretty good.

    Sure have been thinking a lot about that camera shop. Wish I could get back and get started. If I can save five thousand I'll be able to borrow enough more to make it. What I'd like to do is get a partner to put up another five thousand. Did you ever get the bonds I bought while I was at Edwards?

    Haven't heard from Dad for a long time. A letter I sent to him at his first Vancouver address came back unclaimed, so I added a letter and sent it to the address you gave me.

    The Reader's Digest has started arriving. Thank you again for it. The Stars and Stripes has started printing it in four weekly installments, but I would much rather have my own copy.

    Will write again if I have time.

Love,
Bill

X
Out of Time

Bill ran out of time. On January 24 the 142nd again reverted to II Corps control.

142 RTC JOURNAL for 24 Jan 44:

> "Lt. Rogers, 2nd Bn S-2, called. Talked with Maj. Sorenson who gave him what information he had . . .

"25 January 44 . . .

"0930 . . . Lt. Rogers, S-2, 2nd Bn reported to CP . . .

"26 January 1944 . . .

"0745 . . . Lt. Rogers, 2nd Bn, was given the situation on the front by Maj Sorenson."

36 Division, 142nd Regimental records, OPERATIONS IN ITALY, JANUARY 1944:

At 0545 27 January, the Regimental Command Post was established in SAN ELIA, with Brig. Gen. BUTLER, Assistant Division Commander of the 34th Division, also establishing his headquarters at that location.

Roy Caudill's log 27 January 1944:

"Arrived at bivouac area at 2330, approximately five miles East of St. Elia.
Bn. dug in for the night."

OPERATIONS IN ITALY, JANUARY 1944:

The following day, 28 January, was devoted to coordination with the Division on plans of attack and establishing the mission of the 142nd.

It sounds deceptively simple. "[C]oordination with the Division on plans of attack and establishing the mission of the 142nd." It is so much more complicated and dangerous when you realize just how it is accomplished. On the 28th Bill led a reconnaissance patrol across the river. His citation says:

For gallantry in action on 28 January 1944, in the vicinity of **, Italy. Leading a vital four man reconnaissance patrol, Lieutenant Rogers skillfully crossed the treacherous ** River and moved forward over the heavily mined terrain under continuous fire of the enemy. Although pinned down on several occasions by concentrated mortar and machine gun fire, he aggressively continued his advance, cleverly deploying his men and gathering the information essential to his mission. Remaining in this hazardous area until a thorough reconnaissance was completed, he successfully returned to lead his battalion in a swift assault on the objective which he had so capably scouted. Lieutenant Rogers was subsequently killed in Action. His outstanding leadership and magnificent daring were an inspiration to all who witnessed his deeds.

OPERATIONS IN ITALY, JANUARY 1944:

At 0530 29 January, the Second Battalion had arrived and established an assembly area on Hill 382, NORTHEAST of SAN ELIA, which was consolidated into a defensive position later in the day...

Roy Caudill's log 29 January 1944:

"Under heavy artillery fire all morning."

And then it happened.

Feb. 29 - 1944

Dear Mother,

 We are sending the wire from the Gov't with this
letter. I wish Jeanne and I could be with you at this time.
We both feel it very deeply about Bill and extend our
heart-felt sympathies to you. I know how you must feel,
but I know that you will be the brave little soldier that he
would want you to be and bear up. You know that your
son did all he could do for you and his country and you
can be very proud of him.

 We would like to have you come and stay with us and
Jeanne and the boys will go back with you for her visit to
Montana. If it would be more convenient I would be glad
to send you the fare for the trip. We want very much to
have you with us for a visit.

 Jeanne has contacted all the relatives and friends.
Any mail or other communications concerning Bill, sent
here will either be forwarded to you immediately or held
for you as you wish it.

 Let us know if and when you will come and don't
hesitate to let me know if you can use the fare.

Love
Alvin

Jeanne will write later.

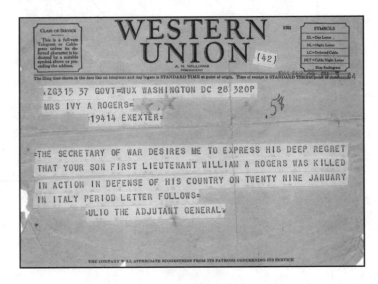

hmc

WAR DEPARTMENT

THE ADJUTANT GENERAL'S OFFICE

IN REPLY
REFER TO AG 201 Rogers, William A.   **WASHINGTON**
(26 Feb 44) PC-N NAT016

1 March 1944.

Mrs. Ivy A. Rogers,
    19414 Exeter,
        Detroit, Michigan.

Dear Mrs. Rogers:

It is with regret that I am writing to confirm the recent telegram informing you of the death of your son, First Lieutenant William A. Rogers, O-1288126, Infantry, who was killed in action on 29 January 1944 in Italy.

I fully understand your desire to learn as much as possible regarding the circumstances leading to his death and I wish that there were more information available to give you. Unfortunately, reports of this nature contain only the briefest details as they are prepared under battle conditions and the means of transmission are limited.

I know the sorrow this message has brought you and it is my hope that in time the knowledge of his heroic service in defense of his country, even unto death, may be of sustaining comfort to you.

I extend to you my deepest sympathy.

Sincerely yours,

J. A. ULIO
Major General,
The Adjutant General.

1 Inclosure
Bulletin of Information.

ddl/1wk

WAR DEPARTMENT

THE ADJUTANT GENERAL'S OFFICE

IN REPLY
REFER TO AG 201 Rogers, William A. **WASHINGTON**
(6 Apr 44) PC-G O-1288126

5 May 1944.

Mrs. Ivy Rogers,

Edgar, Montana.

Dear Mrs. Rogers:

Reference is made to your letter of 6 April, addressed to the Provost Marshal General, and referred to this office for reply, in which you request information relative to the death of your son, First Lieutenant William A. Rogers.

No information has been received concerning the death of your son since the original report which stated that he was killed in action on 29 January 1944 in Italy. I very much regret that the far flung operations of this war on many fronts and over isolated areas and vast expanses of water have served to deny to some of us an accurate knowledge of the passing of our loved ones.

I have transmitted a copy of your letter to The Quartermaster General, Washington 25, D. C., for direct reply concerning his burial, as that official is charged with the duty of the disposition of remains of deceased Army personnel.

May I extend my deepest sympathy in your great loss.

Sincerely yours,

Robert H Dunlop

ROBERT H. DUNLOP
Brigadier General,
Acting The Adjutant General.

XI
The Need to Know

Ivy was not satisfied with the War Department's lack of information. She wrote to Bill's friends Bob Cromwell, Gerhard Rehder, and Charles Stimson to try to find out what had really happened. They all tried to help. Bob Cromwell's letter was first.

Lt. Robert Cromwell
O-1289052
Hdqr. Co. 2nd Regt. Depot
A.P.O. 776
% P.M. - N.Y.C

Italy
May 18, 1944

Dear Mrs. Rogers -
I feel that I know you very well—your son Bill spoke of you so often—and showed me pictures of you—and read bits from letters that you had sent.

I knew your son over a period of 14 months—and we were close as I was his room-mate at Camp Edwards—I was in his company in Hdqs Co. and after coming overseas we never spent a day apart—always together so that where ever you saw him I was there too.

So I knew him perhaps better than anyone else in the entire regiment—his circle of friends was small—and I feel privileged to think that I was one of the chosen few—a Lt. MacIlraith, a Catholic Chaplain, Father Quinn and I made up the small group of men that had access to Bill's thoughts and feelings.

I'm not sure what it was that kept us so closely knit together. Perhaps it was because we shared a mutual love

187

for literature and music and good things of life. Bill had an amazing mind—a mind that ran so far above the ordinary that many people shied away from him because they didn't want to come out second best in a battle of wits. I infuriated him many times because I didn't grasp some deep significance in a book...

He regarded the Germans as an evil thing that must be crushed and eliminated and he coveted the job of S-2, intelligence officer. That was the job he wanted... so it is not difficult to see why he did such magnificent work in that sector when the opportunity presented itself.

I regret that I was not with Bill during his last months. The fortunes of war separated us late in September... I wrote him several letters... the last I had from him dated January 13th, he told me he was working hard and then he spoke of our old days together. I had a feeling he was wishing with all his heart that the nasty business of killing was over. He was a soldier up to the very moment of his death. From first hand reports, I've learned since my return to Italy that he was at his post of duty when the time came for him to go—and that's the way he wanted it—he told me that many months previously "on some hill" he said "in full view of the enemy—that's the way I want it"—and so it was. You have lost a beloved son—and I a beloved friend. God bless him and care for him—always

Sincerely,
Robert Cromwell

Then Gerhard Rehder wrote:

Hq & Hq Sq, 34 Air Depot Group
APO 528, New York, N.Y.
Somewhere in Italy; 24 October, 1944

My dear Mrs. Rogers,

Your letter of September 2nd with the photograph of Bill arrived some time ago, and I regret that I have been so slow in acknowledging it and thanking you for the photograph. It is an <u>excellent</u> one—it is so characteristic and shows Bill just as I remember him. It really seems almost to speak, and I cannot look at it without feeling something closely akin to the warmth of personal contact.

I wish I could answer your questions as to how and where he met his death and where he is buried. But for reasons best known to itself the War Department is rather strict in what it allows one to say. Bob Cromwell actually knows more about the place and occasion, as he had a letter from one of the officers in the outfit and shared a part of it with me. He was killed in the morning, a direct hit, and died instantly, which, if any such thing can be, should be some consolation. An officer near him, with whom he was conversing on business, was wounded. That is really all I know of that. As to his burial place. At the time he was temporarily buried, as had to be done, but he now rests in a military cemetery. I was able, by inquiring, to learn where he was, and last week, on a trip which took me in that area, I went over to visit the cemetery. It is forbidden to name the place or to take pictures, but I can assure you that it is a quiet and beautiful spot, very carefully tended, as are all our American cemeteries. I can't tell you how moved I felt as I stood by the grave and saw the familiar name and the serial number, so close to my own—I often felt that closeness of our numbers seemed to tie us together more intimately in some way—and thought of Bill as I had known him, admired him and loved him. It is a hard thing to get used to, but you know how he would be about it—with that side dip of his head and the mischievous twinkle in his eye—he would laugh at the sentimentality of it all—with a verbal quip or two added. Of course I think he was very soft-hearted and even sentimental at heart—but he liked to poke fun at such things—and I am sure he would be the last one to want others to grow sentimental and sorry over him.

You ask me also where he was in North Africa before he left for Salerno, I'm afraid I don't know, though Bob would, as he was still with the outfit then. I met Bill in Oran first, then he went off into the mountains to the very lovely city of Tlemcen. Later, in late June or July, the outfit returned and were in or near Arzew, near Oran. I

saw Bill last in Oran in July '43 before I left for
Casablanca to join the outfit to which I now belong...

I am sorry that there is so little that I can tell you in
detail, but please do not hesitate to ask me if there is
anything else I can do or find out for you. Once I am back
in the States, and having been over here twenty-six
months, that should not be too far away now, I can write
more freely and perhaps tell you some of the things I
cannot now write of. I live in Boston, which is far from
Montana, but after all the traveling I have done, I should
not be surprised to get to Montana and the west
generally. If I ever do I shall regard it as a pleasant
obligation to pay you a visit, and a debt I owe Bill for his
friendship and affection.

Bill, incidently, used always to call me by my
nickname "Gus," and I should like it if you, should you
write again, would use that more familiar form; it seems
so much more natural in a case like this

> Sincerely,
> Gus

After a long delay, Ivy's letter to Charles Stimson caught up
with him. He answered right away:

> 26th Sept. 1945

My Dear Mrs. Rogers,
I received your letter that you had written to me only
after it was delayed almost a year. I'm sorry that I could
not answer sooner, for I believe that I know how you
must have felt when you did not hear from me.

Yes, I knew Lt. Rogers very, very well. In fact he
joined my company in North Carolina in 1942 & stayed
with us the entire time. "Little Buck" as he was known to
us, tho I believe you called him "Bill," was one of the best
liked officers I have ever known. In a way I might have
called him a personal friend of mine for I still have his
enlisted man's blouse that he gave me before we went
overseas. I spent a great deal of time with him & came to
look upon "Buck" as a very good friend.

He always had a special talent for poetry & seemed able to compose short verses at will. He loved music & anytime he could pick up a bugle or cornet & blast out—he was happy. Also I've often heard him speak of you many times. I recognized your name immediately as soon as I received the letter.

Mrs. Rogers, Buck was Anti-Tank Platoon Leader of our company for many, many months. He served that position fully & was promoted to 1st Lt. around Sept 25, 1943, I believe. He was then promoted to Battalion S-2. In the Army that's known as Intelligence Officer. His job was to secure as much information of the enemy that was possible. Buck was good at that & every one knew it. He had a certain quality that seemed to laugh at danger & back up from nothing. Buck feared nothing, Mrs. Rogers, & I can more than vouch for that. More than once I've seen him tear out through an open space with only a 45 caliber pistol in his hand . . .

Mrs. Rogers, I'm sorry, but I'm afraid that I won't be able to shed much light on Buck's death. You see at that time I was in the hospital recovering from wounds that almost cost me my life. I was hit in both legs & the stomach, but fortunately I made it fairly well. I don't know the exact location where Buck fell, but do know it was on Mt. Cario near Cassino. We lost many men while in that position & gained nothing to show for it. As best I know Buck was hit by artillery & was killed instantly. A good friend of mine who was with him at the time said it all came in an instant & Buck did not suffer a bit. He was struck down while in a forward position doing his job with the utmost courage & ability. I'm not sure of the location that he was buried in, but imagine that it was in our own 36th Division Cemetery near Salerno, Italy. I never got the chance to go back in that vicinity for the company was on the Anzio beachhead when I joined them again.

Again I'll say, Mrs. Rogers, that Buck was a great soldier & a grand guy. It hurt very much when I heard of his death for I knew of no better friend. I'd like so much to help you in any way that I may do so. Please feel free to ask me anything that you like & I'll do my utmost to answer. I have some friends that were near him at the time & will try & find out more for you.

At the present I'm attending college now that my Army days are over. I was discharged late last year & am doing fine now.

Hoping to hear from you again.

Very sincerely yours,
Charles

The actual circumstances of Bill's death were difficult to discover. Regretfully, Ivy died in 1980 never knowing how it had happened. But forty-five years after Charles Stimson wrote that lovely letter to Ivy he still remembers his friend "Little Buck" Rogers. With the help of Charles Stimson, and the 36th Division Association, many of the officers and men Bill served with were contacted. They were generous in sharing their memories too.

Former 1st Sergeant J.B. Worley remembers talking with Lt. Rogers the night before he was killed. Bill had been talking about Montana and a girlfriend. Former Sergeant Jim Henson remembers that Lt. Rogers was killed in the morning. Jim saw the shell hit, but didn't see what happened after that as he was caught up in attending to his own men and their safety and deployment.

Former Staff Sergeant Mabene Allen was wounded the same day Bill was killed. Mabene remembers:

> To the best of my memory he was killed about 9:30 in the morning, just before we secured the mountain. If it had not been for his forward observing we would have lost a lot more men. It was indeed an honor to have known Buck and be a part of the same organization with him.

Some recall events close in time. Former Technical Sergeant Roy E. Caudill, at the time receiving treatment at the Battalion Aid Station himself, remembers:

> The attack was started on the morning of January 29, 1944, and the ambulances and the wounded from the first phase of the attack arrived at the aid station... In talking with the wounded as we moved back to an evacuation hospital I was told the Battalion Commander Lt. Col. Graham and Operations Sergeant Allen had been wounded and that Lt. Rogers had been killed, by a round from German artillery.

Former Second Battalion messenger Johnnie Pricer remembers:

> I happened to be where the officers were gathered and they were telling about the Lt... and we all were very sorry and expressing how we'd miss him and how gutsy he was... We all felt the loss very much because we loved him.

Then a breakthrough. Major John R. Johnson (AUS. Retired) responded to a request for information:

In regard to your request in the May 1990 T-Patcher News Letter for information concerning the death of 1st Lt. William A. Rogers, who was an officer on the 2nd Battalion-142 Infantry Staff, I can submit the following.

I joined the 2nd Battalion-142nd a few days before it embarked for the Salerno, Italy invasion and was assigned to "E" Company as a platoon leader. As platoon leaders in combat seldom meet staff officers, I knew Lt. Rogers by sight and little else. I was transferred to the 143rd Infantry at the Rapido River, along with many others in our regiment. The 143rd had taken such heavy casualties at the river crossing that they needed experienced men to help them continue in combat. My transfer occurred immediately after the river crossing had failed and before the 142nd Infantry was moved to the San Elia sector to the right of Cassino. Upon my transfer, Technical Sergeant J.B. Bunch, who was my platoon sergeant, took over as platoon commander. I can't tell you what day or date this occurred, but within hours of that time, Lt. Rogers was killed ... the same artillery round that killed Lt. Rogers also killed T-Sgt. Bunch.

After the Division was withdrawn from Cassino, I talked to various members of the 2nd platoon of "E" Company, 142nd; and to Captain James G. Barnett (now deceased), 1st Lt. Welden Green, and 1st Sgt. Clifford Hale, all of "E" Company ... It is possible that Clifford Hale and Welden Green are still living, but I do not know any addresses.

Contact was made with both Welden M. Green and Clifford Hale. First Clifford Hale:

Our battalions moved in during the night and were somewhat scattered but were "dug in" on the sides of the mountain. Also dug in, which was actually a barrier of rocks that we built to seek shelter behind since we could not actually dig into the frozen and rocky hillside, was the company's Headquarters Platoon consisting of the various platoon leaders, i.e., officers, first sergeants, runners, etc ... Green, Barnett, Bunch, myself and others. About 15 of us as I recall.

Our position looked down on a mountain road about 200 yards below. And looking south, we could see the abbey on Monte Cassino quite clearly. Early on the morning of January 29th, about an hour after daylight, Lt. Rogers came to our position from Battalion Headquarters with our orders of the day ... Within 15 or 20 minutes of his arrival, three to five tanks came rumbling along the road below us, spotted or assumed our position, and fired several direct hits into us, making instant kills or wounded casualties of our

"Our position looked down on a mountain road about 200 yards below...tanks spotted our position and fired several direct hits into us..."

entire group. Not a single soldier escaped unscathed. So devastating! There were no medicos in the area at all and the aid station was about a mile down through a very rugged area. Finally, three or four of the wounded, including myself, managed to make it to the aid station and stretchers were sent back up for the others. I'm so sorry that I can't recall specifically these moments as they involved your uncle.

Welden Green remembered too:

> We moved up during the night and . . . were sched-
> uled to attack across these high hills in the direction of
> Monte Cassino that morning. In preparation for this
> attack [Lt.] William A. Rogers . . . came from Battalion
> Headquarters to instruct us and coordinate the attack
> and I suppose set the time of attack. Captain Barnett
> and my self were sitting side by side with our backs to
> a terrace. [Lt.] Rogers kneeled down in front of us and
> we were going over the map and planning the attack.
> About this time Sgt. Bunch walked up about six feet to
> our left and asked the Captain about something. As he
> spoke a shell came in, evidently hitting Sgt. Bunch
> direct. When the smoke and dust cleared, all I saw
> was one leg from the knee down laying on the ground.
> [Lt.] Rogers was blown to my right and on his back we
> found no wounds. He evidently died of concussion
> and of course he never suffered.

After Bill's death Jeanne did visit Ivy in Montana. While she
was there, Jean Boyle, Bill's and Jeanne's mutual friend,
enclosed this poem in a July 5, 1944 letter:

When the earth grows warm in the spring
When the mists come up in September
When the Christmas hearth glows and grows dim
We will remember.

Through evil and good to the end
Today and tomorrow
We will add your laughter to ours
Our tears will include your sorrow.

The hour will not come in our lives
When weary, unknowing
We forget the joy of your coming
The grief of your going.

Nor will he ever be forgotten by those who knew and loved him—or those who came to know and love him through reading his letters and meeting his friends.

Bibliography

"Air Transport Command Base." *LIFE* (September 6, 1943), pp. 81-86.

Adams, Henry H. *1942: The Year that Doomed the Axis*. New York: Paperback Library. 1969.

"Battle for the Beachhead." *LIFE* (October 25, 1943), p. 79.

Belden, Jack. "The Beaches of Salerno." *Time* (September 27, 1943), pp. 28-29.

Blumenson, Martin. *Mark Clark*. New York: Congdon & Weed, Inc. 1984.

Blumenson, Martin. *U.S. Army in World War II Mediterranean Theater of Operations Salerno to Cassino*. Center of Military History United States Army. Washington, D.C. 1988.

Bond, Harold. *Return to Cassino*. New York: Pocket Books, Inc. 1965.

Ellis, John. *Cassino: The Hollow Victory*. McGraw-Hill. 1984.

Gilbert, Martin. *The Second World War*. New York: Henry Holt and Company. 1989.

Hapgood, David. *Monte Cassino*. New York: Berkley Books. 1986.

Huff, Richard A. Ed. *A Pictorial History of the 36th Division*. The 36th Division Association. Austin.

Johnson, Robert Erwin. *Guardians of the Sea*. Annapolis, MD: Naval Institute Press.

Kennett, Lee. *For the Duration*. New York: Charles Scribner's Sons. 1985.

Kennett, Lee. *G.I.: The American Soldier in World War II*. New York: Charles Scribner's Sons. 1987.

Lee, Alfred McClung and Norman D. Humphrey. *Race Riot*. New York: Octagon Books, Inc. 1968.

Lichtenstein, Nelson. *Labor's War at Home*. New York: Cambridge University Press. 1982.

Morison, Samuel Eliot. *History of the United States Naval Operations in World War II*, Volume IX. Boston: Little, Brown and Company. 1984.

Morris, Eric. *Salerno*. New York: Stein and Day. 1983.

"Posthumous D.S.C. Awarded." *The Billings Gazette* (September 15, 1944).

Satterfield, Archie. *The Home Front*. Playboy Press. 1981.

Spector, Ronald H. *Eagle Against the Sun*. New York: The Free Press. 1985.

Stars and Stripes World War II Front Pages. New York: Hugh Lauter Levin Associates, Inc. 1985.

The Officers Guide. Harrisburg, PA: The Military Service Publishing Co. 1942.

"The War Summarized." *The New York Times*, XCI (January 26, 1942) 1.

Wagner, Robert L. *The Texas Army: A History of the 36th Division in the Italian Campaign*. Austin: R.L. Wagner. 1972.

Walker, Fred L. *From Texas to Rome*. Dallas: Taylor. 1969.

36th Division Original Records (microfilm, 1965), Archives Division of the Texas State Library, Austin, Texas.

Correspondence to the author:
    A. P. "Pete" Johnson (36th Division Association) (1990)
    Leonard Wilderson (36th Division Association) (1990)
    Charles W. Stimson Jr. (1990-1991)
    Mabene Allen (1990)
    Rudolph Muck (1990)
    Richard M. Rucker (1990)
    Roy E. Caudill (1990)
    Everett S. Simpson (1990)
    Johnnie A. Pricer (1990-1991)
    Milt Winkler (1990-1991)
    Jim Henson (1990-1991)
    Gerhard Rehder (1990-1991)
    Carthel N. "Red" Morgan (1990)
    John R. Johnson (1990)
    Welden M. Green (1990)
    Jack Finan (1990-1991)

Louis Hamilton (1990)
Clifford W. Hale (1990)
Wood Jenkins (1990)
Charles L. Hearn (1990)
G. G. McCullough (1990)
Ralph Leonard (1990)
Evan MacIlraith (1991)
Jean Boyle (1991)
Bettie Lamb Fairbanks (1991)

Interviews with the author:
Jeanne Rogers Shaffer, numerous 1989-1991
Alvin R. Shaffer, numerous, 1989-1995
Donald Bolenske, August 1990, March 1991
Charles W. Stimson Jr., numerous 1990-1995
Jim Henson, numerous 1990-1995
Jack Finan, June 1990, February 1991
J. B. Worley, February 1990, October 1990
E. E. Carter, numerous 1990-1995
Mabene Allen, November 1990
Clifford Hale, November 1990
Terrell J. Davis, December 1990, January 1990
Ralph Leonard, February 1990
Evan MacIlraith, 1990-1995
Gerhard Rehder, January 1990
Charles L. Hearn, numerous 1993

Other Books From Republic of Texas Press

Military History Series

Civil War Recollections of James Lemuel Clark
by L.D. Clark

Henry Ossian Flipper, West Point's First Black Graduate
by Jane Eppinga

Letters Home: A Soldier's Legacy
by Roger L. Shaffer

General Interest

A Trail Rider's Guide to Texas
by Mary Elizabeth Sue Goldman

Exploring Dallas for Children: A Guide for Family Activities
by Kay McCasland Threadgill

Horses and Horse Sense: The Practical Science of Horse Husbandry
by James "Doc" Blakely

Slitherin' 'Round Texas: A Field Guide for People Who Don't Like Snakes
by Jim Dunlap

Women of the West Series

Daughter of Fortune: The Bettie Brown Story
by Sherrie S. McLeRoy

Eight Bright Candles: Courageous Women of Mexico
by Doris E. Perlin

Etta Place: Her Life and Times with Butch Cassidy and the Sundance Kid
by Gail Drago

Outlaws in Petticoats and Other Notorious Texas Women
by Gail Drago and Ann Ruff

Red River Women
by Sherrie S. McLeRoy

Western History and Folklore

A Cowboy of the Pecos
by Patrick Dearen

Cripple Creek Bonanza
by Chet Cunningham

Exiled: The Tigua Indians of Ysleta del Sur
by Randy Lee Eckhoff

How the Cimarron River Got Its Name and Other Stories About Coffee
by Ernestine Sewell Linck

More Wild Camp Tales
by Mike Blakely

Noble Brutes: Camels on the American Frontier
by Eva Jolene Boyd

Santa Fe Trail
by James A. Crutchfield

That Old Overland Stagecoaching
by Eva Jolene Boyd

Tragedy at Taos: The Revolt of 1847
by James A. Crutchfield

Western Horse Tales
Edited by Don Worcester

Wild Camp Tales
by Mike Blakely

Texas History and Folklore

100 Days in Texas: The Alamo Letters
by Wallace O. Chariton

A Treasury of Texas Trivia
by Bill Cannon

Alamo Movies
by Frank Thompson

Defense of a Legend: Crockett and the de la Peña Diary
by Bill Groneman

Exploring the Alamo Legends
by Wallace O. Chariton

Other Books From Republic of Texas Press

Texas History and Folklore (Cont.)

Eyewitness to the Alamo
by Bill Groneman

Ghosts Along the Texas Coast
by Docia Schultz Williams

The Great Texas Airship Mystery
by Wallace O. Chariton

The Last Great Days of Radio
by Lynn Woolley

Phantoms of the Plains
by Docia Shultz Williams

Spirits of San Antonio and South Texas
by Docia Schultz Williams and Reneta Byrne

The Star Film Ranch: Texas' First Picture Show
by Frank Thompson

Tales of the Guadalupe Mountains
by W.C. Jameson

Texas Tales Your Teacher Never Told You
by Charles F. Eckhardt

To The Tyrants Never Yield: A Texas Civil War Sampler
by Kevin R. Young

Unsolved Texas Mysteries
by Wallace O. Chariton

Texas Humor

At Least 1836 Things You Ought to Know About Texas but Probably Don't
by Doris Miller

Cow Pasture Pool: Golf on the Muni-tour
by Joe D. Winter

Don't Throw Feathers at Chickens: A Collection of Texas Political Humor
by Charles Herring, Jr. and Walter Richter

From an Outhouse to the White House
by Wallace O. Chariton

The Funny Side of Texas
by Ellis Posey and John Johnson

Rainy Days in Texas Funbook
by Wallace O. Chariton

Texas Highway Humor
by Wallace O. Chariton

Texas Politics in My Rearview Mirror
by Waggoner Carr and Byron Varner

Texas Wit and Wisdom
by Wallace O. Chariton

That Cat Won't Flush
by Wallace O. Chariton

This Dog'll Hunt
by Wallace O. Chariton